# The Woman with the Artistic Brush

Nikẹ Davies is one of the few African women known internationally in contemporary art circles. *The Woman with the Artistic Brush* traces her life history and illustrates the strategies developed by women to mitigate male rule. Presenting a critique of the woman's place in contemporary Yoruba society from the perspective of a woman who lived it, this book covers Nike's life from the time of her mother's death when Nikẹ was six to the culmination of her dream in the creation, against severe societal odds, of a center for arts and culture that has over 120 members. Along the way, *The Woman with the Artistic Brush* details how Nikẹ ran away from home and joined a traveling theater group after her father tried to arrange her marriage, subsequently married and joined in the polygynous household of a noted artist from the popular Ọsogbo school, and finally broke clear of that situation after suffering sixteen years of domestic violence. *The Woman with the Artistic Brush* is another superb contribution to the Foremother Legacies series.

**Autobiographies and Memoirs of Women from Asia, Africa, the Middle East, and Latin America**
*Geraldine Forbes, Series Editor*

SHUDHA MAZUMDAR
**MEMOIRS OF AN INDIAN WOMAN**
*Edited with an Introduction by Geraldine Forbes*

CHEN XUEZHAO
**SURVIVING THE STORM**
**A Memoir**
*Edited with an Introduction by Jeffrey C. Kinkley*
*Translated by Ti Hua and Caroline Greene*

KANEKO FUMIKO
**THE PRISON MEMOIRS OF A JAPANESE WOMAN**
*Translated by Jean Inglis*
*Introduction by Mikiso Hane*

MANMOHINI ZUTSHI SAHGAL
**AN INDIAN FREEDOM FIGHTER RECALLS HER LIFE**
*Edited by Geraldine Forbes*
*Foreword by B.K. Nehru*

**THE WOMAN WITH THE ARTISTIC BRUSH**
**A Life History of Yoruba Batik Artist Nikẹ Davies**
*Kim Marie Vaz*

# The Woman with the Artistic Brush

## A Life History of Yoruba Batik Artist Nikẹ Davies

*Kim Marie Vaz*

An East Gate Book

*M.E. Sharpe*
Armonk, New York
London, England

**An East Gate Book**

An accompanying video to Nikẹ Davies's life history narrative, titled "Batiks by
Nikẹ," is available from Video and Film Distribution, Student Services Building,
University of South Florida, Tampa, Florida 33620.

**Library of Congress Cataloging-in-Publication Data**

Vaz, Kim Marie.
The woman with the artistic brush : a life history of Yoruba batik
artist Nikẹ Davies / Kim Marie Vaz.
p.    cm.—(Foremother legacies)
"An East Gate book."
Includes bibliographical references (p.    ) and index.
ISBN 1-56324-506-X   —   ISBN 1-56324-507-8 (pbk.)
1. Davies, Nikẹ.
2. Textile designers—Nigeria—Biography.
3. Batik—Nigeria.
4. Yoruba (African people)—Social life and customs.
I. Title.
II. Series.
NK9503.2.N64D3838       1994
746.6′62′092—dc20
[B] 94-22897
CIP

Printed in the United States of America

The paper used in this publication meets the minimum requirements of
American National Standard for Information Sciences—
Permanence of Paper for Printed Library Materials,
ANSI Z 39.48-1984.

BM (c)   10   9   8   7   6   5   4   3   2   1
BM (p)   10   9   8   7   6   5   4   3   2   1

For my daughter,

Iya (Iyamide) Vaz-Kale

# Contents

viii

Fly lit upon glowing brass tray—
    fancied [her]self king
    of reflected glory
Made Ifa for Sacrifice-to-divinity-before-darkness,
    slave of Alapa the destroyer.
Can I get out from under?
Maybe. Sacrifice accomplishes wonders.
What then? Six pigeons, six hens, six shillings, and a bar of soap.
[S]he sacrificed. They fixed medicinal leaves,
    asked [her] to bathe with them, saying
    that all things denied would now be [hers]—
    money, progeny, buildings to house them, fame.
[S]he sacrificed again, had recourse to Ifa regularly,
    and from then on, small jobs brought in big money.
[S]he started building houses to accommodate
    more [artists], more children,
    and people were amazed:
We thought Sacrifice-to-divinity-before-darkness
    was but a slave,
    now look at [her].
How did [s]he come to be
    such an important person?
    and the people said, Ha,
    come and see what this slave has accomplished.
    for [s]he, no [daughter] of the manor,
    has become a local celebrity . . .
    and the people said,
[S]he is fit to wear beads,
    come look at [her] qualifications;
    singing and dancing
    graced with distinction
    come and see how beads would reflect
    [her] authority.

*Greetings for sacrifice offered and received, Greetings!*
[Italics in original.]

    From Judith Gleason, *A Recitation of Ifa, Oracle of the Yoruba*

# Note on Orthography

The orthography used in the book is the style recommended by the Yoruba Orthography Committee. Consonants in Yoruba are represented by these symbols: b d f g gb h k l m n p r s ṣ t w y. The consonant gb has no equivalent in English but the g is guttural and pronounced slightly before the b. The consonant p stands for kp in which k and p are pronounced at the same time. The consonant ṣ is pronounced like the English "sh." Non-nasalized or oral vowels include: a e ẹ i o ọ u. The vowel a is similar to the English "ah." The vowels e, i, and o are pronounced like the long a, e, and o in English and u is similar to the English "oo." The vowels ẹ and ọ resemble the English sound "eh" and "aw," respectively. When n appears at the beginning of a word, its sound is similar to the n in English. Adding an n to the oral vowels indicates that the vowel preceding it is nasalized.

# Acknowledgments

Many thanks are due to Kikẹ Ọdẹyẹmi for her assistance in translation during the interviews with Muniratu Bello in 1988. Thanks to Omiṣore Omiṣakin for his translations during various interviews in Oṣogbo, Oṣun State, and Ogidi, Kawara State. For his fastidiousness in the translation and transcription of all the taped interviews conducted in Yoruba in 1988, for his interest in the project, and for his sheer dedication, I give my profuse and heartfelt thanks to Michael Abiọdun Oduntan. His translation notes were extremely helpful. The following artists kindly granted me interviews regarding the "Oṣogbo School of Artists": Georgina Beier, Suzanne Wenger, and Jimoh Buraimoh, as did scholar Ulli Beier. I am indebted to the senior and junior faculty and staff members of the Faculty of Social Sciences, Ọbafẹmi Awolọwọ University, Ile-Ifẹ, for their generosity and kindness during my stay in 1988.

I am very grateful to the members of the Nikẹ Center for Arts and Culture for the information they provided and for their assistance during my stay in 1990. Particularly, Kings Amao was very helpful with the interviews of Muniratu Bello conducted during that period, as was Gbenga Ọlaniyi, Muniratu Bello's son. There are many Yoruba people from all walks of life who good-naturedly and patiently answered my questions about polygyny and the Oṣogbo artists. I am appreciative to them all. I am grateful to Gerris Farris and Iya (Iyamide) Vaz-Kale for their cooperation and high spirits during the rigorous and frequent travel to the interview sites in 1988 and 1990. My parents, Winston and Lois Vaz, assisted me through their never-failing emotional support and in 1988–89 with their financial support as well.

A generous grant from the Florida Endowment Fund for Higher Education through their McKnight Fellowship program freed me from teaching for the 1992–93 academic year. I was able to bring the manuscript to near completion because of this award. I am delighted that Geraldine Forbes allowed the manuscript to become part of the Foremother Legacies series, and I am grateful for her support. Marianne Bell's clerical expertise was very helpful in printing out drafts of the manuscript. I thank Deborah Plant for her courage and patience during a very trying phase of this project in Oṣogbo in the summer of 1993. Michael Oludare was very helpful as interpreter and cultural consultant in the summer of 1993. Most importantly, I thank Ms. Nikẹ Davies, Ms. Muniratu Bello, and their former co-wives for their trust and candor.

# Introduction

From her first group exhibition at the Mbari Mbayo Club in 1968 in Oṣogbo, Nigeria, to her featured role as one of the more well known contemporary Nigerian artists in the Smithsonian World documentary *Nigerian Art—Kindred Spirits* in 1990, Monica Olufunmilayọ Oyenikẹ (or Nikẹ, pronounced *Nee-keh*, as she refers to herself) Davies has become one of Nigeria's most celebrated contemporary artists.[1,2]

Davies's introduction to art began when she was a teenager, embroidering linen for a local woman tailor in her village. Later on, she began to produce woven cloth using the methods she learned from her great-grandmother, Ibitọla (also called "Red Woman"), who was head of the women's loom guild in Jos in the 1950s. Ibitọla specialized in the production of *ọjas,* long strips of decorative cloth used to carry babies on women's backs (LaDuke 1991). Ibitọla sold her *ọjas* mainly to Ibos for 50 kobo apiece. The sheer labor-intensiveness of this work led her to abandon traditional weaving in favor of the more fashionable *adirẹ*.[3,4] The *adirẹ* proved to be less time-consuming and more profitable. Nikẹ Davies assisted her great-grandmother by drawing designs freehand on the cloth—a typical young girl's task—using a starchy paste made from boiled cassava and alum. The girls used chicken feathers to apply the starch in lines to form squares and then painted various motifs within the squares (Eicher 1976).

Davies learned to embroider, one of the crafts that launched her professional career, in primary school. But neither her work with the woman tailor nor the *adirę* she produced using cassava from her father's farm proved profitable. Having recently completed primary school, and with few prospects for either going on to secondary school or finding employment in her village, Davies left Ogidi to take a position in Kabba as a baby-sitter. With her Sundays off, Davies produced *adirę* using the traditional cassava starch-resist method her great-grandmother had taught her. Her employer routinely showed Davies's work to her friends, and Davies's first pieces were bought for 10 shillings each by two women visiting from Canada. Davies reinvested this money in supplies and made additional *adirę* pieces at the women's request.

While she was working in Kabba, Davies's father, Nicholas Ojo, arranged a marriage for her. Rather than submit to what she considered an undesirable match, Davies ran off with Olosunta's traveling theater and eventually ended up in Oşogbo. Traveling theater groups were organizations founded by an individual who both managed the group and acted in the leading roles of the largely improvised dramas. These groups incorporated comedy routines and songs and dances in addition to the plays. Because their performances were held in different villages or towns almost daily, their travel schedules were rigorous; company members' earnings were scant and irregularly received; and men were the primary consumers of these performances. The community took a dim view of women's involvement in theater activities.

From Davies's narrative we learn about young women's struggles within their own patrilineages that drive them to undertake desperate acts, such as joining socially stigmatized theater groups. A Yoruba father wields an uncanny amount of authority over his daughter—the type and amount of health care she will receive, whether she will be educated, and when and whom she will marry. The father–daughter dyad serves as the archetypal relationship between women and patriarchal figures, where the tenets of male rule are learned and, not infrequently, first defied. The events surrounding arranged marriages often serve as a catalyst for the most contentious encounters between African fathers and daughters. Ojo's decision for an early marriage disregarded the desires and aspirations of his daughter. It was only when Davies and her friend Justina resorted to the drastic measure of running away to join a theater group, whose existence was precarious at best, that their families even inquired into the desires and goals of these young women. Yoruba fathers demand that their children be deferential and obedient, and a young "child is expected to obey the orders of his elders as soon as he is past infant stage" (Fadipẹ 1970, p. 130). Fathers rely on verbal and physical punishment to discipline their children. Nathaniel Fadipẹ reported that it was a common practice for a parent to give a lash to an older sibling to use on insubordinate and rebellious juniors for the purpose of instilling deference to authority. R. A. LeVine, H. H. Klein, and C. R. Owen (1967) interviewed Yoruba fathers and found that even the thought of their children being aggressive toward them "aroused extreme emotion." Such behavior was regarded as "almost inconceivable, warranting banishment or supernatural intervention through cursing" (p. 250). Barbara LeVine (1962) provided evidence that girls were more frequently punished for their verbal aggression toward elders than were boys.

Resistance to male rule is always forthcoming from women reluctant to submit, and men and those women who uphold patriarchal values find it necessary to morally and physically coerce rebellious young women into submission and silence. Christine Froula (1986) wrote that the "hysterical cultural script" is a "cultural text that dictates to males and females alike the necessity of silencing woman's speech when it threatens the father's power. This silencing insures that the cultural daughter remains a daughter, her power suppressed and muted; while the father, his powers protected, makes culture and history in his own image" (p. 623).

This is clearly illustrated by a note of protest registered by a cultural father during the first interview I conducted with Davies's former co-wife, Muniratu Bello. In this interview Ms. Bello described her experiences as an abused wife. An older man, who had been eavesdropping, exclaimed in surprise, "Haa! I hope you know the thing that you are doing is not good." The women present (Davies and a woman university student serving as interpreter, Kikẹ Ọdẹyẹmi) replied, "Look at the men; they don't want the secrets to be revealed."

Fathers' low expectations of women's achievements, denial of education and medical care, threats of forced marriage, unrealistic expectations of the amount of work they can do, disregard for their career aspirations, and verbal scolding and physical beatings can indefinitely sour the relationship between father and daughter. In the case of Davies and Ojo, a redemptive relationship eludes them. In 1990,

when Davies was purchasing her second gallery, she informed her
father that the property belonged to a man who had a university education. She wanted her father to know that she believed her achievement
could have been greater in life if he had supported her educational
aspirations.

Davies developed strategies of resistance based on her interactions
with her father. These were to be expanded and refined over time as
she encountered various expressions of patriarchy within Olosunta's
traveling theater company. Women in Yoruba's popular traveling theater troupes were enmeshed in a pernicious, multilayered patriarchal
system. The oppression and exploitation of women are evident in the
content of plays and in the objectification of women by both theater
managers and audience members. The plots of many of the plays were
sexist. Disgruntled co-wives were often presented simply as petty, jealous women who conspired against their rivals, and urban women were
characterized as bent on financially duping men. These plays, based on
Yoruba lore, were conceived primarily by the men who managed the
groups and acted in the leading roles. These managers and actors often
relied on women's "sex appeal" to entice the groups' mostly male
patrons. The performances were conceived and orchestrated by men
for the benefit of other men. They expressed chauvinistic male concerns, aspirations, and fantasies. Women's images, real and imagined,
were central to these performances.

Yoruba traveling theater groups, whether in cities or in villages,
drew largely male crowds. Judith Hoch-Smith (1978) found that directors, audiences, and actors were predominantly male. The groups performed in front of audiences consisting of "poor wage-earning male
workers whose fathers were rural farmers but whose own aspirations
[were] directed toward the material life-style of the urban-educated
elite" (p. 253). As she made the rounds of nearby villages, Davies
noted that "no women would go out in the evening. Sometimes we
started performing by eight . . . not many women had money to come
in . . . [it was] mostly men who had money. The women would be
indoors or sleeping."

After viewing several plays performed in Ibadan in the early 1970s,
Hoch-Smith concluded that most of them depicted women in roles that
men believed threatened patrilineal social order. Many of these charac-
terizations were associated with women who traditionally are scape-
goated in patriarchal societies: prostitutes, witches, and jealous

co-wives. The male-female relationships as envisioned in these plays expressed men's fear of having their destinies placed in the hands of women, particularly men's fear of women's ability to render them penniless and childless—hence without status or prestige in Yoruba society. At the conclusion of several dramas, Hoch-Smith observed, the male victims of women's machinations had been completely humiliated and destroyed. Women, on the other hand, were portrayed as enjoying the spoils of their victories with their coconspirator female friends. Repeatedly, women were painted as threatening the regenerative powers of men through various mediums of the performance: the improvised script, songs, dances, and costumes. In a Hubert Ogunde* drama, for example, a houseboy warns his employer against "modern" girls, who would change his trousers to knickers (i.e., take him for everything he owned). Ogunde also sang a song about a young girl who did not fetch bathing water or cook, refused to have a second wife, drank, stayed out all night, and beat her husband (Hoch-Smith 1978). The "opening glee," which often delivered a play's theme and moral, also expressed negative views of women. Hubert Ogunde's opening glees often included "'lightly clad girls who go wild on saxophones'" (Graham-White 1974, p. 34). In the opening glee of Kọla Ogunmọla's *Love of Money*, the "trickish" Mopelọla married the physically ugly and behaviorally devilish, though monied, esteemed, and honored "gentleman," Adeleke. Because Mopelọla left Adeleke when he faced hard times, the audience was warned not to trust anyone but God (Adedeji 1973).

Reflecting back on her performance in a play about a senior wife who attempted to murder her co-wife's child, Davies recalled that the play's intention was to chastise a woman for sabotaging her rival's child. She was punished, not because her action was inherently wrong or because of concern for mother and child, but because her action interfered with the patrilineal line of descent and the father's immortality. The play, based on traditional lore and real life, pointed out that "bad" wives are "witches" who must be punished for their offenses. Drawing on her own experiences, Davies refuted the male dictum that "good" wives should cooperate with their husbands, encouraging polygyny and unquestioningly accepting competition for scarce re-

---

*Hubert Ogunde founded the first modern professional theater company in Nigeria.

sources. She saw women's consent to polygyny as coerced and as a weapon used against them when they grow disgruntled with life as a co-wife.[5] Davies recalled an Olusunta theater production wherein a senior wife was cast as a witch:

> They put on a play about a woman who was accused of being a witch. [Her] husband had two wives. She was the senior wife. She was so jealous [that], when their children grew up, she [attempted to kill] the child of the junior wife because the husband loved the junior wife's son more than [he loved] her own. She wanted to [use] medicine to poison the food. The food she gave to the junior wife's son [was poisoned, but he] didn't eat it; . . . her son came before . . . and ate that food. Her son died. . . . [The towns people] made her go to the bush and [they hanged] her. If you kill your junior wife's baby or your senior wife's baby and they find out . . . they take you to the *iroko* tree. The *iroko* tree is very big, just like a baobab. In those days they believed that the woman should [be banished from] the town, . . . and they use[d] her for sacrifice. So as they sent her away to the bush . . . she was singing and crying. They packed her load and made her carry it. . . .
>
> [This] story [is based on actual events] and they [made] it into a play. No woman wants to be [one of] two [wives]. They make you say you want another wife, but it is not from your heart. Women know that it is the pressure. If you agree they will say that you are the one who agreed [that the husband take another wife].

Bíọdún Jẹyifọ's (1984) study of Yoruba traveling theater revealed that the group's founder–leader held a position of preeminence. Founder–leaders "owned" the group materially because they provided the initial capital investment, and they "owned" the troupe intellectually because they contributed most of the ideas for the theatrical productions. Jeyifo attributed the patriarchal structure of the groups to these two factors—and to the organization of the traditional Yoruba family, which emphasizes tradition and hierarchy. Since Yoruba families are patriarchal, the founder–leader's position is assured because he is married to the women of the troupe, and many of the actors are his wives, sons, and daughters. "Family" formation within the troupes was Hubert Ogunde's "solution" to "the peculiar problem" of recruiting female actors. An originator of the theater movement, Ogunde recounted how he came up with his solution. "Now I was able to get some boys, but I was unlucky with the girls. And so . . . I remembered the tradition back home—polygamy is the answer! So I had to keep the girls as wives in order to keep going on" (cited in Jeyifọ 1984, p. 81). And, with this solution, Jeyifọ concluded, "Ogunde has justly become famous and imitated" (p. 81).

The community viewed women who belonged to these troupes as undesirable, thus adding another layer to the oppressive forces operating in this theatrical arena. Because of the stigma attached to female troupe members, founder–leaders encountered numerous obstacles in recruiting female actresses. As a result, many group managers married the women in their troupes. These men encouraged their wives to recruit and help to retain other women by having the wives extend offers of marriage on behalf of their husbands. The men were successful at this in part because the amount of work wives had to perform was burdensome, and women were looking for some relief. Also, men pressured their wives to conform to their wishes by threatening to divorce them. The women's lives were made even more difficult by the rigorous traveling schedule and the uncertainty of drawing an audience large enough to enable the actors to be paid their wages, which would in turn assist them in consistently obtaining nutritious food, ensure there was a place to sleep other than the performance hall or space itself, and make available money for transportation from one village to the next; otherwise, the troupe walked from site to site, carrying many of their props on their heads.

Women in the theater were frowned on by their communities. Jeyifọ wrote that contempt for a theatrical career was expressed most strongly with regard to women. Hubert Ogunde relied on a strategy of expedience that became famous—to marry his actresses to keep them within the troupe. Jeyifọ suggested that since this strategy became popular with the majority of the other founder–leaders of the movement it was a testament to the difficulty of recruiting and retaining female actors. That Ogunde's solution had negative consequences for women is seldom, if ever, discussed. The issue in question is one of the plights of women with tenuous family ties contracting work and, later, marriages, to assure some modicum of economic stability—with men who in turn demand that they participate in recruiting female labor through the offer, not of wages, but of legitimization vis-à-vis marriage. According to Davies, a female member of the Yoruba traveling theater was seen as a "poor woman who has nowhere to go and . . . no other means of surviving or living":

> so they count [the woman] as somebody [banished] from [her] family['s] house. The man [leader of troupe] now wants to marry any woman that comes in, and [he tells] the wife—[uses] the wife—[instructing the wife by saying], "You have to go talk to her. You have to make sure you tell her you are going to look after her." The woman is not really happy to approach another woman for her husband. But [she has] to do it; if not, the husband could say, "I am finished with you." That is why the woman keeps saying, "I want you to marry my husband."

The basic structure of the traditional Yoruba family involves hierarchy and authoritarianism, and those same attributes characterize the internal relations of the traveling theater troupes. Jeyifọ contended that, just as within the family, the oppressive and burdensome aspects of patriarchy within the theater group were significantly lightened by the "genuine solicitude" and paternalism of the leader (and those lieutenants he privileged above other members) to the rest of the troupe. In addition, over time, the troupe members developed "corporatist" sentiments because the work schedule on the road tours involved sharing in all the hardships and hazards the troupe encountered. And because of the demanding work, many wives contracted marriages for their husbands. As Davies stated:

> Women in the theater would try to [get] another woman [to marry] their husband. [In] this theater, [women] carry a [heavy] load. They want [other women] to share the work with them. They want the husband to have another wife [so they can do] less work. They tried to marry Justina, who was my good friend. She had breasts. I didn't have any breasts and they said they wanted to marry her—this is the two wives of the theater man. Justina kept thinking, why should she marry them? Then they said, "We want you to stay with us; you are beautiful. You are lovely. We want our husband to marry you and we are not going to get jealous." Justina [agreed] to marry them, but when the wives thought she had slept with the husband they were not happy. I told her, "You know we [did not] leave home to marry. As soon as he makes you pregnant you are going to be in trouble." Justina said she would not let the man go to bed with her. She just accepted [the marriage proposal] so they would . . . [look] after us well. She accepted the offer but she never went to bed with the man.

Jeyifọ's idea of "genuine solicitude," while true in many families, is one that may not hold for some women in the theater. It is the absence of solicitude in the family that is often the primary reason why women run away from home to join socially disparaged groups and then run away again from the theater troupes to even more precarious existences. 'Mọlara Ogundipẹ-Leslie (1992) recently pointed out that all sexism is negative and undesirable, irrespective of how it is labeled, because "benevolent" sexism is usually one expression of the more malignant forms.

Jeyifọ (1984) wrote of the risks troupe members were exposed to and the arduous life they faced. Uncertainties regarding food, accommodations, and health services coupled with constant road tours added up to a hand-to-mouth existence. A diet of *gari* and *akara* balls was common.[6] For those troupes successful enough to have buses or lorries, breakdowns in the middle of "nowhere" presented other obstacles. For members of troupes without their own transportation, carrying items upon one's head was the rule. "We were really struggling. Some places we [went] there was no food. We [got] any little thing we could get from the farm and [cooked] it, and some places we [drank only] *gari* for the whole day. We would trek to the next place, and nobody would come [to see the plays]. It's a [great] struggle." Although desertions were high, members could become accustomed to the life. When Davies was ready to leave the theater, her friend Justina did not want to go. She had gotten used to the life.

In the Yoruba traveling theater movement of which Davies became a part, women acted out parts that were derogatory to them but beneficial to male founder–leaders, whose aspirations included validating their male audience's hopes and fears. Founder–leaders could take advantage of polygamy to somewhat ensure a relatively stable labor pool. Wives of these men were often forced to collude in this inequitable setup because their own position within the theater "family" could be threatened by noncompliance.

Woman-centered theater and the questioning of male prerogatives was instituted in one of the few troupes founded and led by a woman.[7] Funmilayọ Ranko, a former boxer who competed against men, founded her troupe in 1968. Unlike male founder–leaders, Ranko found it easy to recruit women, and they became the stable members of her company; men came and went. Ranko conceived the plays herself, focusing on social issues of the day, and she acted in the leading roles. When only women began to perform the cabaret-style dances in her opening glees, she stopped performing such dances herself and limited her own dancing to ritual occasions when called for by the drama. Although stigmatized women were portrayed in the productions of this troupe, men were made to suffer for their disrespectful arrogance toward women, and women came to varying ends, not just those involving feminine coconspiratorial glee. In one of Ranko's plays, a woman used her family's resources to educate her husband abroad. When he returned, his friends told him it was no longer fashionable for an educated man to be married to an illiterate. Embarrassed in front of his friends by his wife's housekeeping, he sent her away, much to the dismay of his own parents. When his lover stole his company's money and his expensive furniture, he was crushed and returned to his parents in remorse. His parents, who had been sheltering his wife and children, informed him that they would locate his wife for him only if he promised to humbly prostrate himself before her—which he did. This ending caused quite a commotion (Jeyifọ 1984).

In addition to her other creative occupations, Davies has been contemplating sponsoring a drama on Nigerian television protesting the physical and emotional abuse of women: "The story is about a woman who has no job, and [whose] husband . . . beat[s] her all the time. . . . One woman come[s] and say[s], 'Why don't you . . . take an office job?' So she [takes] the office job and she [has] a little money. When the politic[al movements begin] she join[s]. . . . [Eventually] she [becomes] a senator. [Her] husband cannot beat her anymore."

Davies left Olosunta's group to go to Oṣogbo because of the physical hardship: Her move to Oṣogbo was to prove pivotal in the shaping of her career. In the 1960s, various artists, notably Georgina Beier, ran workshops in Oṣogbo "to produce local artists to serve the design needs" of the emerging Duro Ladipo National Theater (Jẹgẹdẹ 1994, p. 31). The "Oṣogbo School of Art" (1964–66), as it came to be called, emerged from the Mbari Mbayo Club established by Duro Ladipọ with the support of Ulli Beier. Ladipọ returned to Oṣogbo, his hometown, in 1958, after teaching in northern Nigeria. He first established the Popular Bar in his compound and ran the Ajax Cinema. He founded a small theater group consisting of students from the Grade 2 Teacher Training College at Oṣogbo. The group performed a Christmas cantata on Ibadan television in December 1961. After this success, Ladipọ began to write historical plays and compose and perform church music. In 1962 he founded the Duro Ladipọ National Theater Company and opened the Mbari Mbayo Club on Oṣogbo's main road (Beier 1991).

Ulli Beier, then the University of Ibadan's resident extramural tutor at
Oṣogbo, decided that Ladipọ's Mbari Mbayo Club, with its "reservoir"
of potential artists (actors and musicians), was an ideal place to hold an
Oṣogbo art workshop designed to provide opportunities for local
residents who had "no preconceived ideas about art." The Mbari
Mbayo Club's location in Oṣogbo, Beier suspected, "would draw curi-
ous passers-by into the workshop" (Beier 1991, p. 63). The first
Oṣogbo workshop was conducted over a five-day period by Guyanese
painter, novelist, and art historian Denis Williams in 1962. Williams
held a second workshop in 1962 in conjunction with African American
artist Jacob Lawrence. Ladipọ company members Jacob Afọlabi and
Rufus Ogundele attended the workshops and continued painting after
the workshops ended. Georgina Beier, who had recently moved to
Oṣogbo and set up her studio, assumed the task of mentoring both
men. In 1964 Georgina Beier conducted a third workshop, at the end of
which "several artistic personalities had emerged: Twins Seven Seven,
Bisi Fabunmi and Muraina Oyelami," who were also part of Ladipọ's
company (Beier 1991, p. 68). Although the Beiers worked primarily to
develop the talents of male artists, some men passed on these contemporary methods to a few female apprentices or wives in the men's
polygynous households. Davies initially worked as an apprentice to
one of these artists before becoming his wife.[8] Her husband was one of
the first men whose talents were "developed and supported by the
workshops and the publicity which followed" (Butler 1986, p. 72).
Davies noted that she was able to become a contemporary artist only
because she was married to one. Without such contact it is unlikely
that her work would have been exhibited at the Mbari Mbayo Club in
1968. Davies's chance opportunity suggests how African women's
participation in contemporary art is severely restricted by Western and
African patriarchal practices. Davies's success and her life as an artist
were often made difficult by the physical, sexual, and emotional violence that her husband inflicted on all of his wives.

Women as apprentices and artists in their own right have been left
out of the discursive formations of Oṣogbo art. The tremendous
woman-power that energized many of the Oṣogbo artists is yet to be
acknowledged. It was not unusual for these men to employ women to
perform the tedious work of coloring in their sketches or filling in the
outlines of their drawings with embroidery. For example, Bisi Fabunmi
produced five hundred sketches and hired female sewing apprentices

to complete the embroidery. His art was a joint effort between himself and women, although this is not the way he represented it: "I made the drawings on the black cloth and took them to a sewing mistress whose girls didn't always have enough work. I chose the colors and told them which stitch to use. Then I paid them for each panel. I sold my first embroidered picture to Jean Wolford for £10. That encouraged me and during the next few years I produced about 500 embroidered pictures" (Beier 1991, p. 34). Davies's first husband "laid his wives' hands to art" in this way. Even those who had no interest in art before coming to live with him learned to color in his sketches.

Beier (1991), for example, never even mentioned women in his catalog written for the exhibition "Thirty Years of Oṣogbo Art," which was sponsored in part by the Goethe Institute in Lagos. This is very odd, since Beier discussed the "multiplicator effect" of the Oṣogbo School—or the emerging artists who were directly influenced by the handful of men who constituted the original membership. By 1991 Davies had received worldwide recognition as an artist and had been successfully training young artists for years, first at her home and then, since 1988, at the Nikẹ Center for Arts and Culture. By 1991 Davies had emerged as one of the most visible and successful descendents of the Oṣogbo School progenitors.[9]

The few women who have had some indirect access to the training provided to the men, such as Alakẹ Buraimoh, Davies, and Abimbọla Akerele, were confined to the production of textile art, a medium traditional to Yoruba women. Fortunately for women, textile arts have proven to be a more lucrative medium than, for instance, stone carving and aluminum paneling. One advantage of textile art is its moderate price. Also, since the fabrics produced can be used in a variety of ways, it has the widest patronage (Jẹgẹdẹ 1984). Men in the Oṣogbo Art School, however, work in a variety of mediums (e.g., carving, sculpture, batik, embroidery, brass casting, and painting) using a variety of materials (e.g., beads, broom straw, glass, paper, cloth, wood, and stone). For example, Yekini Fọlọrunṣọ produces panels describing Yoruba religion and secular life in brass, copper, and aluminum. Joseph Ọlabọde, Davies's brother, produces scenes on boards using colored beads. Isaac Ojo tells traditional stories based on Yoruba religion in hand embroidery. Father and son sculptors Jinadu and Kasali Ọladepọ create small-scale works, such as staffs and jewelry cast in brass alloy (Zamana Gallery 1988).[10]

Although the workshops in Oṣogbo were open to men and women, women's productive and reproductive responsibilities obligated them to spend their time earning a living; hence, few women attended the workshops. Moreover, there existed a social stigma regarding the nature of this new art and theater with its emphasis on Yoruba religious lore. The artists were regarded as "mad" persons and "pagans" (Armstrong 1981). The social pressure against participation in the theater and the emerging art movement was widespread and most intense with respect to women.

Due to the sexual division of labor among contemporary Nigerians, men have a monopoly on professions that recommend them to media such as sculpting, which can facilitate their entrance into the realm of "fine arts." Men therefore bring their diverse backgrounds to bear on their contemporary training. A number of men, such as Adeneji Adeyẹmi, Tijani Mayakiri, Bayọ Ogundele, and Muraina Oyelami, incorporate their experiences in the theater as actors, musicians, and dancers into their current artistic productions. Many of the men who worked with artist Suzanne Wenger (an Austrian-born artist and priestess of Ọbatala) in what she has called "sacred art" had other occupations prior to being commissioned and encouraged by her in reviving the sacred groves in and around Oṣogbo. These men were well positioned to innovate on their professional work, using contemporary techniques, and indeed were sought because of their professional expertise. For example, stone carver Buriamoh Bgadamọsi was originally a carpenter and aluminum panelist; Aṣiru Ọlatunde was a professional blacksmith and jeweler (Zamana Gallery 1988).

As one of the few well-known contemporary women artists, not only in Oṣogbo, but in Nigeria, much of Africa, Europe, and the Americas, Davies has stirred—and sustained—an interest among the international press. Writing for the *Lagos Weekend*, Dele Ọdẹbiyi opened an article about Davies on this note: "In contemporary Nigeria, Fine Arts seems to be almost an exclusive preserve for the menfolk. . . . However there is one woman whose parental upbringing and marital luck has placed her in the right perspective, not only to become a sung artist but also to serve as a link for our cultural heritage and contemporary arts" (1981, p. 8). Women are not widely represented in contemporary Nigerian art, according to Ọdẹbiyi, "because doing art seriously involves sacrificing time for thinking. It also entails moving around, learning one or two things which form the bulwark of subsequent artistic expressions" (p. 8).

Ọdẹbiyi's observation points to women's heavy domestic responsibilities, which do not afford them the luxury of time for extended reflection. Davies noted in an interview with Denton, Texas, news reporter Elise Gibson (1981) that women's domestic responsibilities, which include participation in the market economy, preclude many Nigerian women from becoming artists. "A woman's household duties, which include trading, take too much time for most women to pursue art" (p. 1B). Referring to Davies's needle batiks, a reviewer for the *Guardian* observed that "the needle is transformed by Nikẹ Davies from an ensign of feminine domesticity to a tool for asserting the prowess of the woman in a male-dominated community of artists" (Staff 1985a, p. 10).

Underscoring the long, hard struggle for women artists in Nigeria, Davies once told *Calgary Herald* reporter Sherri Clegg that "women have a very hard time in my country. . . . They do all the work and the men collect all the money. There isn't time to develop their talent" (1987, p. E4). Davies noted that, although being a wife of an artist made it possible for her to become one herself, her growth as an artist was compromised in part by her domestic life; Davies separated from her husband, calling it "breaking away to success" (p. E4).

**Motifs of Davies's Batiks**

Like many Ọṣogbo artists, Davies finds the origins for her designs in Yoruba religion and folkore. For example, the dazed drunk in her work entitled "Palm Wine Drinkard" is based on the famous Yoruba tale of a man who follows his palm wine tapper into the world of the dead. Folklore often coalesces with personal observations and experiences to poignantly express Davies's concern for women's suffering. Through batiks such as "Breastless Blind Woman," "Mother of Africa," and numerous works on the sacrifices to the female deity Ọṣun, Davies provides a commentary on ideologies and practices that keep women's "eyes cast down." The stories told in the evening by the older women in Davies's village often spoke to issues surrounding women's constrained position. The batik entitled "Breastless Blind Woman" is a sublime representation of one such story. It depicts the determination of a woman to have a full life, even though she was born both breastless and blind. According to the story, the woman decided she wanted to become a performer and ignored the protests of family members. In

Davies's village, people who had physical deformities or physical disabilities, or both, were kept indoors and denied participation in any social activities.

In an interview with me, Davies articulated the ideas expressed in her "Mother of Africa" batik: "Women normally suffer more. Women must carry their loads on their heads, and no one will take care of their children if they are left behind. Anywhere [women] go they have to take the[ir] children, because they have no help."

By depicting a woman as a "talking drummer" in one batik, Davies visually documents an aspect of women's activities not ordinarily recorded. As Davies's comments suggest, it is often social pressure, rather than customary and contemporary laws, that prevents women from participating in many public aspects of Yoruba life. In the case of talking drummers, men prefer to maintain this sphere for themselves. There are families in which women are talking drummers, but they generally are not sought out to perform at traditional ceremonies. Davies attributes this to men's use of public performances as a vehicle to meet and woo women. Men's resistance to women's public participation, Davies charges, is their attempt to control women's sexuality: "Whenever these musicians go out they meet women, but they don't want the women in their families to meet different men. They don't want women to play the drums because they know that men will be looking [at them] and [pursuing] them."

Davies's numerous batiks representing the worship of the female deity Ọṣun are informed by her sense of the power the Yoruba attribute to this deity. According to Davies, Ọṣun's power is "so big and so strong" that before people undertake any type of activity in the face of adversity they consult her. When women want to have children they carry sacrifices to the Ọṣun River and promise to make more sacrifices to Ọṣun in return for the gift of fertility.[11] Having protected the Yoruba township Oṣogbo from the invading Fulani warriors during the nineteenth-century campaigns, Ọṣun became Oṣogbo's revered heroine and remains so today. Warrior, orişa,* mother, wife, worker, teacher of Ifa divination to other women, giver of children, and comforter of barren women, Ọṣun mythologically embodies both power and femininity in the eyes of her worshipers (Badejọ 1989).

---

*The orişa are the goddesses and gods of Yoruba religion.

## Techniques, Exhibitions, Workshops, and Collectors

Davies has gained worldwide fame through her imaginative and skillful production of batik art. Working with various materials from cotton to silk, Davies begins by drawing a design on the fabric. The design is then traced using melted wax applied with a sponge brush cut to a sharp point and tied to a stick. The fabric is then dyed. More wax is applied to areas of the fabric where the first color is to be retained. The process is repeated until all the desired colors are added. Generally, light colors are added first to avoid bleaching the cloth, a requirement when dark colors are added first. The final color is the blue-black of the indigo dye, a "signature color" in *adire* and batik. Next, the cloth is boiled in large industrial drums; this process strips away the wax and sets the dye. The cloth is then rinsed in cold water and hung to dry. Davies works with both imported synthetic dyes and natural dyes derived from vegetables, flowers, and tree bark (Porrelli 1983). Although this wax-and-dip sequence is the basic technique, Davies varies the procedure. The wax-and-dip method has the disadvantage of limiting the artist to six or seven colors. In a method she calls "waxing before tracing," Davies first waxes the areas on the cloth where white will appear, then applies various dyes directly to the cloth. After the dye dries, more wax is applied to the dyed areas and the whole batik is dipped in indigo. The artist can use as many as twenty different colors with this method, and Davies often adopts it when she works with vegetable dyes, as that kind of dye is not plentiful. In a second variation, "tracing before waxing," the artist paints the entire cloth first, then forms the design using wax. The cloth is then dipped in indigo dye.

Davies's batiks vary in size (smaller pieces are two feet by three feet; large-scale works are five feet by eight feet) and price (from $25 to several thousand U.S. dollars for large wall hangings).

Two other mediums Davies has employed, though less frequently because they are so labor-intensive, are needle batik and embroidered wall hangings. In needle batik, "the cloth is folded, stitched, and tied before dying so that when the threads are removed, figures are made. Delicate touches of embroidery are then used to form important details of the image" (Scott 1983, p. 47). Davies's versatility does not end there. Much of her early local (Nigerian) acclaim came through her work as a fashion designer for Nigerian women, as well as through the numerous institutes and embassies in Lagos, Kano, and Kaduna that regularly held exhibitions of her batiks. Early on in Davies's career, her work was so well respected that at an exhibition held to celebrate Nigeria's independence her work was singled out by then-president Shehu Shagari.

Davies had her first overseas workshop in 1974 at the Haystack Mountain Crafts School in Maine. There, as a weaving instructor, she taught men and women the Nigerian art of making *ojas*. The Tribal Art Gallery in New York sponsored an exhibition of her work the following year. Over the next few years Davies exhibited throughout Europe. In 1976 her work was exhibited at the Commonwealth Institute in Edinburgh, Scotland. In 1979, Davies represented Nigeria at an international arts festival in Stuttgart, Germany, and in 1980, her works were displayed at the Oxmann Art Gallery in Holland. Davies's notoriety in Europe was followed by growing interest in the United States and Canada. In 1981, together with her brother, Joseph Ọlabọde, and good friend Victoria Scott, Davies exhibited her works at the Stewart Gallery in Dallas, Texas, the Denton Unitarian Fellowship Hall in Denton, Texas, and the Malcolm Brown Gallery in Cleveland, Ohio. In 1982, her art was exhibited at the American Museum of Natural History in New York City. In 1983, she held workshops under the auspices of the Los Angeles County Fair's Fine Arts Exhibit "African Images in the New World—Magic, Myths and Visions." Davies participated in an educational program organized through Canada's Institute for Development of Education through the Arts (IDEA) in 1985. She toured schools and gave workshops on batik art, and in August of that same year she participated in the Edinburgh Festival in Scotland, which highlighted Oṣogbo artists. She was featured in the *Boston Globe Magazine* in January 1986, and her photograph graced the front cover.

Embracing the political cause of women, Davies attended the United Nations Decade for Women Conference as part of Nairobi's African Heritage Gallery's exhibition of African women artists. Other exhibitors included Kenyan potter Magdalene Odundo, Ugandan textile designer Grace Ochero, and Swazi women weavers. Davies also was the guest of honor at a ball sponsored by *Viva*, a women's magazine, during the Nairobi conference (Staff 1985b, p. 10). In 1986 Davies began her association with and support of Akina Mama wa Afrika (Solidarity among African Women), a London-based group that highlights the struggles of peasant and working-class women in Africa. Its objective is to study and respond to matters that affect African women by supporting women's organizations in Africa, linking them with charitable trusts and voluntary or public bodies (Kanyogonya 1986). In March 1986, Akina Mama wa Afrika and the Africa Center organized a month of activities that focused on various aspects of women's lives. Davies led workshops during Akina Mama wa Afrika's conference "Speaking for Ourselves," and the center exhibited her works.

In 1988, Davies opened her own gallery, called the Oṣogbo Artists Cooperative, in Oṣogbo, Nigeria, along with several male professional artists. In 1989, the Oṣogbo School was featured in an exhibition at the Zamana Gallery in London. Davies's ability to mediate between galleries and local artists is clear, as she is listed in the acknowledgment section of the catalog from the exhibition. December 1990 found Davies participating in a special exhibition, which coincided with the book launching of *African Ark: People and Ancient Cultures of Ethiopia and the Horn of Africa* (1990) by photographers Carol Beckwith and Angela Fisher at the African Heritage Gallery in Nairobi, Kenya. Recently, Davies was featured in Betty LaDuke's (1991) *Africa through the Eyes of Women Artists*. In July 1992, Davies participated in Die Zweite Internationale Litfass-Kunst Biennale, an international exhibition of graphic artists in Munchen, Germany. There she exhibited her largest work, consisting of fifteen separate panels, titled "Discovering the Past."

Collectors of her work include former U.S. vice-president Walter Mondale; the late Jomo Kenyatta, former president of Kenya; former Nigerian president Shagari; the National Council for Art and Culture, Nigeria; the Museum of Chicago; the Bank of Chicago; and the Smithsonian Institution.

**Origin of the Study**

I met Nikẹ Davies in August 1988 at her home at the Ido-Oṣun junction along the Old Ẹdẹ Road, between the towns of Oṣogbo and Ẹdẹ in Oṣun State, Nigeria. We met quite by accident. I was conducting research for my dissertation on mixed marriages between Yoruba men and Western women. Someone suggested that I go and see Davies, as she might be a good informant. She was in the opposite situation—that is, she was a Yoruba woman married to a European man. In our initial meeting, she began to recount the story of her first marriage to a Yoruba polygynist and felt that it would not be good for me to interview her without interviewing all of her former co-wives. Obviously, we were talking about different subjects, but I was so intrigued by her story and inspired by her success that I began a second project.

Davies introduced me to six women with whom she once shared a husband. With the exception of two, all of these women were engaged in the production of batiks; one was an independent contractor and the other was an independent seamstress at the time. All had divorced their common spouse. I conducted unstructured interviews with these women and some of their older children between August 1988 and January 1989. The interviews with the co-wives often took the form of discussions between two of the women. Each woman affirmed what the other said and served to rouse the memory of the other. This mutual validation and assistance also took place in the interviews wherein one co-wife interpreted for another who did not feel proficient in English.

To gain the background necessary to understand these life histories, I interviewed people who had insight into Yoruba customs. I found Timi of Ẹdẹ (the king of Ẹdẹ, a nearby town), an elderly trader in Oṣogbo, women living in neighboring villages, and ex-girlfriends of the co-wives' first husband to be willing conversants. I traveled to Ogidi to meet Davies's father and to see the village where she grew up. To understand the origins of the Oṣogbo artists, the related sacred art movement, and their impact on the local community, I interviewed Ulli and Georgina Beier, Jimoh Buraimoh, and Suzanne Wenger, as well as Davies's first husband.

I returned to Nigeria in the summer of 1990 to conduct further interviews with Davies and her co-wives. Three of the women I initially interviewed were out of the country. I focused my research on Davies and Muniratu Bello because of their intriguing stories and the possibility of carrying out comprehensive interviews with them. Two of the co-wives were hesitant to participate because they thought relating their stories would tarnish the reputation of their former husband. They based their fear on exposure of their private lives in Nigeria's widely read gossip paper, *Prime People*. This fear undoubtedly was generated by Davies's discussions about her life with her former husband in the local newspapers. Her former husband would often reply to these articles by consenting to an interview to refute her charges. Davies engaged in the exchange, reasoning that in order to be free from the tyranny of fear engendered by the husband's threats it was necessary to challenge his perspective and his interpretation of their marital lives. To remain silent was to remain ensorcelled. Davies's determination to "set the record straight" is the primary motivation for telling her story here in *The Woman with the Artistic Brush.*

Davies's co-wives requested that their names be withheld. I refer to each one, with the exception of Muniratu Bello, by her place in the order of matrimony in the compound (e.g., the first wife, the fourth wife). Although anyone remotely familiar with Oṣogbo art will quickly identify Davies's and Bello's first husband, Davies and I made a conscious decision not to use his name.[12] Davies is still referred to in Oṣogbo and in some reviews of her work by her first husband's surname. She is seeking an independent identity, and the use of her name only in her narrative will further her goal in strengthening her sense of autonomy. Davies also feels antagonistic to the man who caused herself, her children, and her former co-wives enormous suffering. She explained her feelings of having him remain unnamed in this work in this way:

> Talk about your enemy and don't mention his name. He will be so hot that he will put his finger in his mouth and bite it. Blood will never come, even as he bites it ferociously. He can bite it to death, but the blood will never come. In other words, you don't ask your enemy to die. Your enemy can be alive while you are making progress right in front of him, and he can't do anything to stop it. He will regret all the bad things he has done to you because he never knew you could become something.

Davies's second husband declined to be interviewed and became a minor stumbling block for the project. He felt that women were easily beguiled by men, and that I, being a woman, would simply listen to her first husband's side of the story and write from his perspective. What he feared was not clear to me. His refusal to be interviewed progressed to attempts to prevent Davies from meeting with me altogether, so Davies and I agreed to conduct the interviews during his working hours or when he was out of the country.

After reading over interviews with Bello that had been transcribed and translated by research assistants from the Nikẹ Center, and after I had transcribed all of the interview material with Davies, I returned to Oṣogbo in the summer of 1993. The Nikẹ Center had grown tremendously. Signs of emerging affluence among the artists abounded. Many owned cars and were building houses. Several had traveled abroad. A dance troupe with drummers had been added. The building Davies bought in the summer of 1990 had been refurbished and turned into a gallery. Numerous cars, station wagons, and vans had been purchased and labeled with the Nikẹ Center logo. Davies was also building a large guest house next to her own home. The number of Nikẹ Center members had increased from forty in 1990 to more than a hundred in 1993. Signs were placed along the highway and in strategic places in town directing visitors to Davies's studio and gallery. I went over the narratives with both Davies and Bello to obtain fuller explications of data from earlier interviews and to clarify my own understanding of Yoruba culture and society.

I organized the narrative chronologically beginning with Davies's childhood and ending with her polygynist marriage. Thereafter the organization switches to themes and accomplishments: domestic violence, life as a co-wife, the origins and growth of her career as an artist, her thoughts on "strong women," and the Nikẹ Center for Arts and Culture. Bello's narrative is organized chronologically. As the editor of these narratives, I have remained true to their intent. I have changed verb tenses in cases where clarity would be jeopardized, and where it might inhibit readability I changed forms of words. For example, "pregnated me" would read in the text as "impregnated me." In no way do these textual changes misrepresent what Davies and Bello have conveyed to me.

Aspects of an individual's life history that are highlighted not only include what the narrator deems important but also are determined by what fascinates the interpreter or what she sees as important. The interview questions are guided by what the interpreter finds compelling. In my own case, I am profoundly struck by the incredible resilience of Bello and Davies; Davies's genius as a businesswoman; and the warm friendship and reciprocity of goods and services that continue among Davies, Bello, and several of the women with whom they once shared a husband. My interview questions emphasized the community the wives developed among themselves and their resistance to patriarchal oppression.

## Herstory

Nikẹ Davies was born in the early 1950s in the farming village of Ogidi, eight kilometers from the town of Kabba in Kwara State, Nigeria. The destiny of most female children in the village was to marry,

bear and care for children, attend to the daily domestic duties of cooking and cleaning, fulfill extended family responsibilities, assist in the
preparation of traditional or other religious festivals as well as naming,
marriage, and funeral ceremonies, and engage in the production and
selling of various foodstuffs, such as palm oil and cassava.

As the daughter of a peasant farmer, Davies became aware early in
life that the reason for her existence was to provide additional labor
and income for her family's household economy. At the age of six, she
began her career in trading, selling leaves from banana trees to women
who prepared food to sell for immediate consumption. Consequent to
her mother's death, while Davies was still only six years old, she found
herself faced with the burdensome and routine domestic responsibilities that ordinarily fell under the jurisdiction of a mother. Somewhere
in a day, she attended primary school.

Coming of age as a woman in Ogidi in the mid-1960s often meant
forgoing education; this ensured illiteracy and exclusion from more
prosperous and less laborious occupations. It also meant marriage to
older men who already had two or more wives. Marriage to such men
and the lack of education virtually ensured that a woman's future
would be bridled with poverty and its attendant sufferings.[13]

After completing primary school, Davies went to work as a baby-sitter
for an Indian family who lived in Kabba, a nearby town. She dreamed
of using her earnings to pay her secondary school fees. She also hoped
her father might add to her savings to help facilitate the achievement of
her goal. Ojo, however, had already arranged a marriage for her daughter with a local civil servant who was financially well off (as compared
with the majority of the community residents). Ojo intended to use his
daughter's "bride-price" to obtain a wife for his only son.[14]

This arranged marriage proved objectionable to Davies; she therefore chose to defy her father and tradition. She ran off to join Olusunta's traveling theater group. She supported herself by performing in
the troupe's shows and by carrying out servile tasks for the group such
as fetching water and carrying the troupe's props on her head as they
moved from town to town, often on foot. She also supported herself
with odd jobs such as carrying concrete for construction workers.

Davies left Olusunta's troupe to work as an apprentice for an Oṣogbo
artist. In 1968, hoping for a refuge and a place to develop as an artist,
an unsuspecting Davies fled to what she would soon discover was a
chaotic compound. She expected to meet the artist Suzanne Wenger

there, whom the man who was to become her husband suggested would assist her in becoming a contemporary artist. Instead, Davies became an apprentice to this man, her husband-to-be, coloring in his sketches, performing as a dancer for his band, trekking from house to house to sell his artwork, and assisting his first wife with their young child. Underpaid by the artist, she continued to pick up odd jobs such as carrying concrete at building sites. That the artist saw her as sexual prey is borne out by his repeated attempts at and eventual success in raping her. Because of her sense of community with the women who became part of this artist's polygynous unit; for the sake of her own children, the first conceived during her rape; and as a result of her dedication to the various art forms she was able to learn and master, Davies remained for the next sixteen years part of a family whose existence revolved around providing entertainment and works of art for expatriates in Nigeria and affluent African visitors to their compound in Oṣogbo.

During her tenure in her first husband's compound, Davies estimated that between 1970 and 1986 as many as fifteen women either lived there as wives of her first husband or cohabited as if they were his wives. A group of seven wives formed the nucleus of the family. Also in residence were the women's children, their husband's mother, and the members of their husband's band, as well as his apprentices. Because of the camaraderie that grew among the wives in assisting each other with their domestic responsibilities and their constant companionship, which deterred loneliness and mitigated the painful remarks and machinations of an abusive spouse, Davies saw her story as a shared one and strongly urged me to speak to all of these women. Seven of the former wives that I interviewed indicated that they had been physically and psychologically abused. Beatings and sexual assault were most likely to occur when their husband had been drinking. Another reason Davies suggested that I interview her former co-wives was to establish the veracity of her own story. In Oṣogbo and in the minds of many expatriates there existed a perception that the family was fairly harmonious, an illusion the wives admittedly perpetuated themselves. Indeed, the family was described to me by a member of an expatriate community near Oṣogbo as an example of "a beautiful polygamy," and many Nigerians I spoke with were surprised by the extent of the women's mistreatment. For the sixteen years that Davies lived in the compound, she and the other wives experienced repeated violence, some of which involved husband and wife, and some of which involved just the co-wives. The acts of violence perpetrated by Davies's first husband included sexual assault, physical beatings, and threats. He also withheld money for food and medical care, verbally denigrated the co-wives, occasionally showed each one some amount of preferential treatment, and requested that the wives engage in lesbian sex and in serial sex with him. The state of polygyny, intensified by the husband's deleterious practices, engendered in the women a fierce competitiveness that compelled them to engage in whatever tactics might secure resources for themselves and their children and assure them the husband's affection and sexual attention. Among the co-wives there were physical fights, an attempted poisoning of a child, accusations of witchcraft, and verbal abuse through song.

The climate of violence and terror that existed in the compound also included theft of food, clothing, and money by the members of the band, the apprentices, passersby, and hangers-on. The band members and the apprentices often acted as instruments of their leader's domination. They reported on the women's activities and carried out acts of violence against others who assisted the wives in their attempts to earn money.

Davies devised a variety of strategies to negotiate patriarchal rule from her position as a co-wife.[15] The first was the manner in which she secured herself financially. As her husband did not like his wives to leave the compound, Davies sought the assistance of her brother, Joseph Ọlabọde, and her friend Victoria Scott to distribute her batiks to various customers and embassies. This was necessary because any profits from the works sold from their home went to her husband. In a second strategy aimed at gaining freedom of movement, Davies accommodated her husband's unreasonable requests, constantly reminding herself that jealousy toward other wives and concubines would only earn her a dose of her husband's malice. As she traveled, she visited women whom her husband wanted to marry. Sometimes she traveled without her husband's permission; on her return she would prostrate herself before him and beg his forgiveness. Then, too, her husband would not be so hard on her, because she was a ready source of cash for him. Davies often lent him money from her own bank account, all the while leading him to believe she had borrowed it from the bank, incurring personal debt on his behalf.

A further strategy involved Davies's coalition with her co-wives. "We grew up together. It was like being in a girl's school," the seventh wife recalled as she and Davies sat in the latter's home for the interview.

Each wife had strengths that contributed to the personal and economic development of the others. Davies's forte was in marketing not only her own batiks but those made by her co-wives. Davies indicated that her former co-wife Muniratu Bello was the first to divorce their husband, leaving him and her four children.* This was incredible to the other co-wives, who felt that he had a metaphysical viselike grip on them.

Muniratu Bello began weeding and planting crops on her father's farm when she was four years old. She also performed the ordinary housework of girls her age: carrying water from the river to be used in the production of palm oil and shelling cocoa from the pods and transporting it by foot to a nearby market for wholesale. Bello was still in primary school when her menstrual period began, but the Islamic custom that a girl should not have her second period in her father's house led her father to arrange a marriage for her with a local imam (Muslim prayer leader). This imam had several wives and children already and would have required Bello to dress in the full veil worn by Muslim women in that part of the country.† Like Davies, Bello rebelled against her father's authority and the proposed marriage and ran away from Ogidi to the compound where Davies was living as a co-wife.

An additional strength of Bello's that endeared her to Davies was her loyalty as a friend. For example, during the traditional ceremony in which Davies's eldest son received his tribal marks and circumcision, custom held that an adult receive an incision using the same knife, still wet with the infant's blood. Davies refused to consent to have her own body cut. Bello stepped in and "took the boy's pain."‡

---

* Traditionally, Yoruba men retain custody of the children upon divorce.

† Yoruba Muslim women wear the jelubaba, a black veil which covers the entire body.

‡ Sympathetic scarification is performed during an infant's circumcision or excision and cicatrization to remind the parents to handle the child gently, and the Yoruba ethic of communally sharing pain is expressed through these serial incisions. Body marks are used extensively among the Yoruba for purposes of communicating biographical information about wearers, such as their professional affiliation and for reasons of beautification, effecting medical cures, expressing grief over the loss of a loved one, and for protection against malignant forces. This surgical field is the province of body artists called *oloola* (meaning "those who make marks in human flesh"). Enduring the pain of body marks allows the wearer to enjoy social admiration. Body marks are evidence of an individual's courage and strength (Drewal, 1989). That Bello withstood these incisions is not only proof of her friendship, but also an act of bravery that is consistent with her self-image.

Bello was often the object of the co-wives' petty tyrannies. These sometimes became outbursts of extreme jealousy and rage. Bello found herself
involved in physical fights with the co-wives and recalled one co-wife's
attempt to poison her child. In Bello, their husband found a convenient
scapegoat. Not infrequently, when another co-wife's child died, their
husband accused Bello of having *aje** and using it for evil purposes
because none of Bello's own children ever died.[16] Subjected to bodily
mutilation, starvation, poor medical care, and rejection at the hands of
their husband, Bello is described by the other co-wives as being their
husband's most disliked wife. Consequently, she suffered more than
any other of the co-wives.

Davies credits Bello with becoming a role model for the women and
showing them the value of autonomy. Bello's courage to rent her own
apartment and leave her children at their husband's compound set
an example for the other co-wives to plan for their own marital
dissolutions.

The fourth wife taught her co-wives about "releasing" during
intercourse (i.e., having orgasms) as a necessary and pleasurable
part of their sexual lives. The fifth wife was strong—the daughter of
a hunter. Not only did she stand up for herself when the husband
wanted to beat her; she defended the other wives against him to the
extent of physically fighting him. She put her fierceness at Davies's
service when the latter was scared to build a house and buy a car
without their husband's permission. The sixth wife had an affair and
discovered that their husband was not omniscient as he had repeatedly claimed. The co-wives had feared that he would be able to tell
when they had been with other men. She convinced them that he
would never know, and hence each of them had lovers from that
point on.

Taken together, the co-wives' stories illuminate a praxis of self-
help; a process whereby a group of women unlearned rivalry and
worked toward a harmony that ultimately resulted in the discovery of
their individual talents and made possible the sharing of these strengths
within the community of co-wives.

---

*Aje* refers to preternatural abilities which can be possessed by men or women.
The accusation of the negative use of these abilities is primarily leveled against
women.

## The Nikẹ Center for Arts and Culture

At the Nikẹ Center for Arts and Culture women and men are trained and nurtured free of charge in various visual art forms (*adirẹ*, appliqué, pen and ink on cloth and paper, batik, quilting, beadwork, wood carving) and in drumming and dance. Reporter Curtis Walcott has observed that through her center, as well as her gallery, Davies is preserving the traditional techniques for creating *adirẹ* cloth, passing down old technology to a new generation. Davies suggests that the craft is very much in decline because it is time-consuming (sometimes requiring weeks or months to complete) and without sizable economic return. Moreover, the cloth is no longer fashionable. Parents prefer that their children attend school to prepare them for occupations in which they will earn salaries, not become artists. But because she markets her students' works throughout Africa, Canada, Europe, the United States, and the Caribbean, Davies is overcoming major economic challenges of supply and demand. In March 1992 the African Heritage Gallery in Kenya mounted an exhibition featuring only work from the Nikẹ Center for Arts and Culture, which now represents 150 professional artists and artists-in-training. In a recent article in the *Christian Science Monitor*, Robert Press (1992) fittingly described Davies as a teacher devoted to African art. By acting as a liaison in establishing exhibitions and promoting the sale of Nigerians' works, Davies links Nigerians to the world and the world to traditional Yoruba customs.

Many writers and reporters stage Davies's struggle as an intrafamilial conflict between herself and her first husband, but Davies's life has been spent negotiating partriachal systems at every turn: first in her father's house, then in Olosunta's traveling theater, in her first husband's compound, and in her marriage to a European man whose patriarchal worldview is tinged with racism, and within the male-dominated Oṣogbo art community in which she has emerged as a most charismatic figure and influential businessperson. From Davies's initial defiance of her father to the subversive, income-generating methods she adopted during her first marriage, she has continuously broken with the regressive aspects of contemporary Yoruba social norms. Davies recalls with pride that she was one of the few women in Oṣogbo to don trousers. As an entertainer, she learned to play the guitar for an all-male band. On stage she performed, cross-dressing, in comic skits, pretending to be a man.[17] She again broke with established practice and became a cement supplier to local builders.[18] With the substantial earnings she gained from the sale of her batiks, Davies purchased a Volkswagen Beetle, making her one of the few women in Oṣogbo to own a car. Today, she is a leader in Oṣogbo, and the rules governing her center reflect her moral vision for economic empowerment of women and youth. Davies is committed to women's progress and is an ardent opponent of women's economic slavery and the subordination of women through the institution of polygyny. Through her nonprofit organization, the Nikẹ Center for Arts and Culture, she hopes to reach local women and give them opportunities for earning a living beyond the low-volume retail trade.[19] From Davies's narrative emerges a picture of how the successful navigation of male-defined institutions is a function of the interplay between a woman's understanding of Yoruba patriarchy; her ability to stand in solidarity with the officially unempowered (i.e., her co-wives) and to identify and use the strengths of this woman-centered community; her participation in a profession that is economically profitable; and a self-confidence that could withstand daily sexist (and racist) assaults.

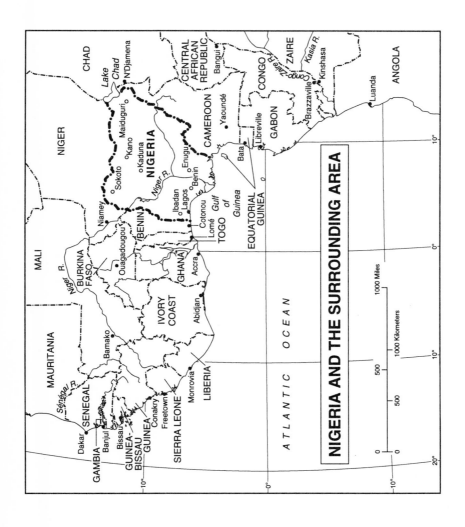

NIGERIA AND THE SURROUNDING AREA

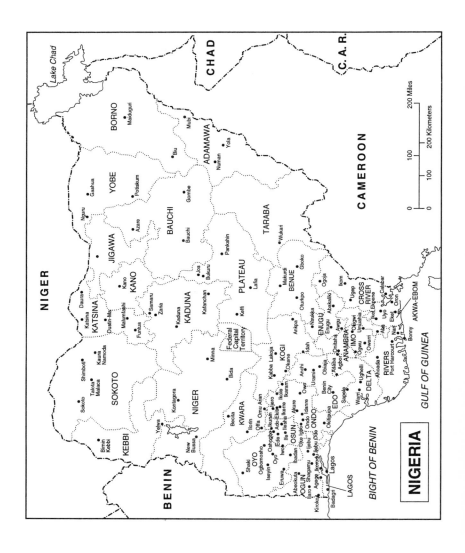

# The Woman with the Artistic Brush

# 1

## "Come and Buy Leaves!"

My mother, Mary Jogolẹ, was a strong and hard-working woman. She was a weaver, with her mother, and made *gari*, a favorite food in Nigeria.[1] She embroidered pillowcases and tablecloths. She always said, "I want you to have good clothes. I want to work hard even if I don't have more than two of you. I want to make sure that you are well cared for."

The day she died, she just lay down, saying she had a headache. During the night family and neighbors called me and said, "Come and look at your mother." I looked and was surprised. I didn't know someone could just die like that. It was very painful. I didn't know what to do. I just cried. When the mourners came to the house they all cried. That is our people's custom; they just keep you crying for a good five days.

When my mother died I didn't know what killed her. She just went to sleep and never woke up again. In my village there was no hospital. The villagers believed that an enemy killed my mother. In my society, when we did not know what caused a person's death we suspected that the person had an enemy. We believed this because there was no good medical care. But as I grew up I learned that enemies couldn't kill a person unless they poisoned you or used something to spoil your blood.

I went to stay with my grandmother, who was called Ọranuiyawo. She was the second to the last wife of her husband. She was hardworking too. During my year with her, she always petted me and made me feel good. She cooked all my meals and made sure I had clothes on my back, but she was in a lot of pain; she kept saying that all the children from her late husband were dying—one every year. Oranuiyawo was one of fourteen wives. Her husband had been the king of the town and was entitled to many wives. He kept marrying more, trying to have a son. Only his last wife had a boy. After the death of their husband, most of the wives went back to their parents' house. When I went to live there, just four or five wives were living in the late king's house. My grandmother was not happy at all. I think she died because she worried a lot about my mother's death. She was very healthy, but she cried constantly. I stayed with my grandmother, but I visited my father. I did not live with my grandmother permanently as I was supposed to because my father's house and grandmother's house were close by.

My grandmother died one year after my mother, and my grandmother's sister, the senior member of the family, took care of me. On the day of Oranuiyawo's death, the women relatives made me a big meal. I did not understand. I kept asking for my grandmother. They told me that she had just passed away. I asked how she could pass away just like that. My grandmother's sister consoled me, saying not to worry, she was my mother now and she would take care of me the way my grandmother had. But still, I couldn't feel really comfortable with her as I had with my grandmother. They buried my grandmother in the palace. I remember that while some were digging the grave, others were dressing her up.[2] They dressed her in gold chains and nice clothes. She was placed where everybody could see her. The good cloth that she had never even worn was buried with her. I thought that they could have given some of it to me. I did not have any clothes to cover myself, and the ants were just going to eat it anyway.[3] In Yoruba society, the family waits before dividing the deceased's property. By the time they divided my mother's and grandmother's property, I was left with only one wrapper. From this point on I began to suffer.

My father, Nicholas Ojo, did not want to remarry, and many people thought this odd. He had had only one wife in all his life. One woman thought that maybe he was impotent. Others accused him of not having enough money for the bride-price. Still others said that no woman would marry him because he was too wicked. In fact, he is a bit hard on women.

My father used to work for the king, and the king rewarded him by giving him my mother. The king could have given him either land or money for a bride—just one, but not both. My father already had land. He had planted cocoa and coffee, but it takes a while (sometimes more than ten years) for these crops to yield a harvest. He was making a little money from his farm, but the crops brought in very little. My mother did not want to marry a farmer. Her father had to force her to marry him. She was not happy, and my father always referred to the fact that there was not much love between them.

To bring in extra money, my father made marriage baskets. It took him five days to make one. He used the money to pay his taxes. Taxes were high, and some men who could not pay theirs left town and stayed at their farms. If they had come back to town they would have been arrested. Things were better when my mother was alive because she sold her weaving. Any little money she made was used to prepare soup to make sure we were fed. We got only one outfit a year when my mother was alive.[4] When she died, I did not get even that.

I was seven years old when my grandmother died. My father still had not remarried, so I went to live with my great-grandmother, Ibitọla, in Jos. My great-grandmother was very healthy. She ate a lot of vegetables and worked on the farm.[5] When she was a young woman she left her husband to start a new life, so she moved to Jos from Ogidi. She had not wanted to marry the man in the first place. In her time, when women married, they were told by their parents, simply, "Tomorrow you are going to your husband's house." Ibitọla protested. She told her parents that she would never go to bed with the man because he already had three or four wives. Her family arranged to have her taken to the man's house by force. Her husband's friends helped him to rape her. They held her legs and body tight while he entered her. She left her husband then and went back to her father's house, but everyone told her she had to marry again. She decided that she would never agree to marry someone in her village, so she left three months later. For a time, she lived with a man from Ogbomọsọ. After some years, she still had not had a baby, so she went to live with another man, from Ogidi. My grandmother was born from that relationship. Ibitọla and the man from Ogidi stopped getting along, however, because the man brought another wife into the house. My great-grandmother went back to the man from Ogbomọsọ, who eventually got another wife when my great-grandmother started getting old.

When a Yoruba woman begins menopause, her husband thinks she cannot go to bed with him anymore, and he uses this as an excuse to take in other wives.[6] The woman, however, still wants to be close to her husband. He tells her, though, that if she had intercourse with him, she would become ill. His semen would stay in her belly because her period would not be there to expel it. This is a man's idea. Men think that a young woman will make them young again, and women just accept it.

My great-grandmother came to Ogidi when my grandmother died. The women relatives prepared a lot of food for her, adding meat and fish to the soups. I ate with her and was so happy. I said to myself, "I am going to follow this older woman anywhere she goes." She said, "You are my great-granddaughter and I am going to take you to Hausaland." At that time I had never left the village. The day she told me I was going, I stayed up all night packing. I really had nothing to pack except a little basket my father had made for me. With the wrapper I got from the division of my mother's property Ibitọla made me a dress; that was all I had. I had no shoes; I always walked barefoot. Ibitọla also made me underpants from a wrapper and used rope to tie them on me.

I was on top of the world when I got to my great-grandmother's compound in Jos. In my village there was no electricity, but there was in Jos, not only electricity but so many vehicles and people dressed in different ways.

I was so excited, and I had many new experiences in Jos. My great-grandmother cooked for her husband twice a week. She boiled meat and then gave me some of the bone to chew. Her husband said, "You are teaching this girl to steal. If you give her meat now, and later on you don't give her meat, she will steal it from the pot."[7] My great-grandmother said, "I have to look after her. She needs [the meat] to make her teeth strong."

The local children taught me to speak Hausa, and the local people loved my great-grandmother. Her neighbors prepared food for me just because I was her great-granddaughter. Ibitọla was a weaver, and she made me a loom out of a calabash to teach me. It took me a while to learn, but after two months I was allowed to work on the regular loom.

For extra money, my great-grandmother collected leaves and put them on a tray; I would sell them. I went around the village with the older people, saying, "Come and buy leaves!" Most of the people who bought the leaves were those selling cooked food.[8] All cooked food was wrapped in leaves because there was no plastic.[9] The trays we carried on our head were made from wood. They were very heavy. My tray's weight was three kilograms. After a while, the hair in the middle of my head stopped growing, and I became bald. The place where the tray rested was like a big callus. It looked just like the arm of those who play the talking drum—right above the player's wrist there is a thick black line. No blood goes there, but the callus goes away when they stop playing the drum.

Children were ashamed to have to sell things to the public.[10] It meant that their mothers could not afford to care for them. When someone wanted to buy what you were selling they called you over. They might begin to abuse you and insult you. They might send you away because they felt your product was too expensive. If you got upset easily or lost your temper quickly, you would not be successful, because people always tried to reduce your prices. Some sellers elevated their prices so the buyer had to wrangle with them until they agreed on the price. I was always ashamed to sell things to the public, but I had no choice. People would say, "Come, leaf seller." A whole load of leaves would bring 5 kobo. If the leaves were small the buyers would hold one in their hand, look at it, and then send you away without buying. I always made sure my leaves were large enough to be satisfactory, and I did not inflate my prices. That is how I avoided the abuse. I never liked to argue too much, and I was always ashamed of this work. Even so, I have sold things all my life. When I finally went to live with my father, he would tell me to sell the animals that he had killed on his hunting trips and bring him the money.

My great-grandmother called me aside one day when I was eight years old. She said, "Your mother died at a young age and I don't know whether she had you circumcised." She looked between my legs and gasped. "This is dangerous," she said. "You have not been cut. We have to do it." She called the people who made Yoruba tribal marks in Jos.[11] They made me undress and lie down flat on my back. The man who performed the circumcision was about sixty-five years old. He looked at my clitoris and commented that some are long and some are short, "but we still have to cut them." He pulled my clitoris and cut the tip off. It started bleeding. He used his fingernail to tear the skin. Then he used a razor to cut the remaining part around the edge.[12] I was screaming, and he scolded me saying that little babies don't even cry. Imagine watching somebody cut your body and having them say,

"Don't cry."[13] He said the wounds would heal in five days, but that was not true. Every morning after that, I sat in warm water. My great-grandmother applied charcoal and other medicines to the wounds. She poured palm oil on cotton and wiped it over the cuts. It took between one and two months to heal. Every time I urinated I felt so much pain. I use to hold my urine for an entire day at a time.

Most girls were circumcised when they were about to marry or when they were about two months away from giving birth for the first time. The theory behind this was that the wound would heal together with the vagina after birth. The pain from birth and the pain from the circumcision would go together. If there were many girls to be circumcised, they were put in a house together and circumcised at the same time.[14] I was circumcised early because my great-grandmother said she did not know whether or not she would be dead before I grew up and was about to marry.[15] She wanted to protect my future. If a woman was not circumcised, it was believed that no man would marry her.[16] Also, my great-grandmother did not want me to have bad luck when I had my first child. If the head of the baby touched the tip of the clitoris, the baby would die. We so much believed this.[17]

After some time, my great-grandmother and I traveled from Jos to Ajowa, where my father's brother lived, to attend my father's mother's funeral. The funeral ceremony of my father's mother was a big affair. My father's mother belonged to the group that worshiped Imalẹ—a female earth-spirit in Ogidi's traditional religion.[18] We buried my paternal grandmother on the third day after she died. Some time after the burial, we held a wake. On that day, the people in the village carried a coffin throughout the village, crying out, "Now is the time for you people to see she has children." Her children and their whole families had to come out of their houses. The villagers danced and introduced each of her children. They said, "This is grandchild number so-and-so." The purpose of this tradition was to show that after death there was still something to celebrate. The people said, "She did not die without having children. Come and see her children." The group that worshiped Imalẹ believed that anybody who died who had been involved in the group's rituals should have these traditions carried out.

During the celebration my father gave me 10 kobo. It was so much money; I didn't know what to do with it. I bought eight sugar cubes for 1 kobo. I gave the sugar to my friends and told them I was also celebrating my grandmother's death. My father's brother bought cloth

and gave each child two yards. All the children had to be in uniform.
The adults took out a carved wooden staff and danced around it on
behalf of the deceased. We sang, "Our mother died. She is gone for-
ever and she will never come back again."

Her contemporaries performed the traditional dances. A group of
women gathered together and wore *ojas* on each of their wrappers.
They did not wear headwraps; instead they wore their hair loose. The
members of the secret societies performed their own dances. Then the
masquerade began.* The children, grandchildren, and great-grandchil-
dren of my father's mother painted their bodies red with *osun*,† which
comes from a tree and is used to make people's skin light. It does not
bleach the skin, though; it has no soda in it. All the children who had
not reached the age of marriage were completely naked. We put on lots
of beads. On regular days, girls who were grown up covered their
breasts, but on the day of the festival, everyone saw them. Girls who
already had pubic hair put on more beads to try to cover themselves,
but it never worked. People could still see everything. Then we
danced through the village, singing, "I have nothing to hide. You
can look at it; it's not hanging down."‡ The ceremony lasted five
days.[19]

After three months the family divided my grandmother's property.
My father said that he did not want anything and that all that was to go
to him should be given to me and my brother. All that they gave me
was a piece of cloth and a basket my father had made for my grandmother. The basket had a cover, so I used it to hold my money and
personal things.

By this time I was nine years old, and my father's family felt that
my great-grandmother was too old to care for me on her own. The
family used the occasion of celebrating my grandmother's death to
convince my great-grandmother to move back to Ajọwa in 1959. In
1960, my father's brother registered me for school. Prior to that, I did
not go to school because students were not permitted to enroll in the

---

*Masqueraders embody both the ancestral spirits and orişas and represent the
ancestors among the living. Masqueraders are believed to be able to use the power
from the spirit world to deliver the people from illness and misfortune (Arẹmu,
1991).

†The bark of the Pterocarpus Erinaceous or African redwood yields a red dye
and is used when camwood is scarce (Abraham 1962).

‡"It" refers to the clitoris.

middle of the year. What was worse, however, was that I had to start all over again from where I left off in Jos.

We lived with my uncle in Ajọwa, and I began to use his name. He was so nice to me; I used to think he was my father. They called me Olu Akẹju.* The people in Ajọwa were set against my great-grand-mother. They criticized her for leaving her own people to go and live with the Hausa.[20] She replied that the Hausa were friendly and honest and accepted her like their own sister. She had been the head of the weaver's association in Jos; everyone liked her. She was chosen to lead the craftswomen there, becoming the *iya-ẹgbẹ*,† because her work was the best. She was teased fondly in Jos, called "the woman who is red," because she was so light in color.[21] But in Ajọwa it was too crowded; we lived with too many people. Everything caused fights among the women in my uncle's compound. There were six families in one house, and some of the wives always fought with my great-grandmother.

We had to find our own food. My great-grandmother and I went to my uncle's farm, but we could only gather the palm kernels that the squirrels kicked off the trees and those that lay on the ground. My great-grandmother did not own the trees, so we had no right to what was on them. Our own relatives would not allow us to cut palm kernels from the trees. We collected some five palm kernels from under one tree, and we went from tree to tree with the same results. We could only make enough palm oil to last for two or three days.

On one occasion, we ran out of firewood. When we went to the farm I said to my great-grandmother, "Take some of this firewood." "It is not yours," my great-grandmother said, "it is for your father's brother's wife, and I don't want somebody younger than me to be abusing me." "If you don't take some, I will," I said, "because I helped her to get it." When my uncle's wife went to the farm the following day, she noticed that some of her firewood was missing. My great-grandmother told her that I had taken it. The woman became angry and began to scream at my great-grandmother. I cried that day. I had cut that wood, and we could not even use enough to make a fire for one night. I thought to myself, if my mother were alive, I would not be working for someone else's mother for nothing.

---

*God's generosity.
†The female leader of a society or group of women.

That woman, my uncle's wife, thought of my great-grandmother as an enemy. My great-grandmother was the senior-most woman in the compound, and if she died, this woman would be the head. She wanted my great-grandmother to die quickly so that she could take over. To hold the senior position is very important. When a goat is killed, the senior-most person gets all the best parts. My great-grandmother said that when she died, even if this woman put 50 kobo down for the ceremony, it should not be used.

My uncle's two wives fought between themselves. Each wife slept with my uncle for a period of five days. During that time the one sleeping with him would cook for him. When it was the other wife's turn, she would say, "It is my time. You had better take your mat and go out." They would sing songs of abuse to each other. One would sing, "If you divorce my husband, I will have a chance to claim your room. If my husband permits me I can dance and shake on top of him." The other would sing, "You think I am going to leave my husband so you can use my room? No way." The husband had no right to ask the senior wife for anything when it was the junior wife's turn. Even if her husband did not actually sleep with her, the one whose turn it was would be on top of the world. That was how it was until the senior wife died a few years ago.

One time, the junior wife became pregnant by her husband's brother. My uncle was so upset that he stopped speaking to both wives. He wanted to chase them out of his house. The senior wife scolded the junior wife, who caused this problem, saying, "I have never done anything against my husband since he deflowered me. I have not been with any man." "If your husband does not go to bed with me, I have the right to sleep with another person," the junior wife retorted. "You are the one who has taken our husband and you will not allow him to do anything with me." My uncle stopped providing food for us, and the wives stopped cooking. One day, though, the whole family was called together. The elders sacrificed a big goat. After the sacrifice and after the junior wife's baby died, my uncle calmed down and there was peace in the compound.

In general, my uncle was kind to the children. And when we were not fighting, I enjoyed living with him in Ajowa. Every Saturday we went to my uncle's big sugarcane farm. He cut pieces of the cane and gave us children as much as we could carry, telling us to eat as much as we wanted and sell the rest. There were three other children my age living in my uncle's house: his daughter, his brother's child, and a friend's child. We four sold the cane at the market. Uncle took half of the money and we kept the rest. Cocoa season was a happy time too. We shelled cocoa beans and left them to drain in a calabash while we went to the market. When we returned, we drank the liquid. It was sweet like sugar and because it intoxicated us, we called it the "wine of cocoa."

During a time when everything was okay and I was very happy, one of my uncle's sons called me to him. "Monica, you naughty girl," he said, and then he gave me a knock on the head. "You go to your father." I did not know what I had done. All the while I had thought that my father's brother was my father. I cried. When everybody left the farm that day, I stayed behind. I did not want to go home with them because I was so upset. I sat around for about an hour afterward, wondering what my cousin had meant. My uncle had never said that I was not his child. I knew as I sat there thinking that my great-grand-mother was going to be upset with me because I was late. I decided to pluck cayenne pepper to use in the dinner soup. I got to the place where I was going to gather the pepper, but the brush had covered the pepper plant. I did not have a cutlass with me, so I used my hands to uncover the plant. I got to the bottom of the pepper plant and saw a big snake. Fortunately the snake was sleeping. I was lucky not to have stepped on it. I was so scared that I did not know what to do. I had no weapon with me. What could I use to kill a snake? I had been taught to break the back of the snake first so that it could not get away, but I had nothing even to hit it on the head with. I ran and fell down and got up and ran again. I kept thinking that the snake was going to follow me. I thought to myself, if I had known, I would have gone home with those people. I thought it was the end. I ran all the way home, and I never stayed behind again.

Every month on the farm, we killed a male goat and cooked it with palm oil and pepper. We also cooked soup and beancakes with no palm oil. Without the oil the cakes were very light. We had a sacrifice to ensure productivity of the cocoa trees. This is called an ẹbọ. We ate some of the food and we distributed the rest throughout the farm, calling to the spirit of the farm to come and eat.* By observing ẹbọ we

---

*The patron divinity of the Yoruba farmer is Orisa-Oko.This divinity embodies both masculinity and femininity since the deified ancestors who comprise Orisa-Oko were husband and wife. Orisa-Oko's communion feasts are especially sumptuous (King 1986).

believed the trees would continue to give much cocoa. My uncle had plenty of sugarcane, pineapple, and cocoa. I enjoyed my life there.

I had been living in Ajọwa for three years when my father came and said I had to go with him to Ogidi. I started crying and said that my uncle was my father. I believed this was so because I was registered at the school under his name. I asked my uncle which one of them was my father; then I learned who my father was. By that time I was twelve; I could cook, wash my own clothes, and do most things for myself. I was in primary grade four in Ajọwa, but I had to start primary grade four all over again when I went back to Ogidi. I had no one in Ogidi to look after me when I went to school. I had to do everything myself. My father woke me up at five in the morning because he went to the farm very early. I swept the house, fetched water for drinking, then walked about two kilometers to the well to fetch water for bathing. I used a little bucket with a cover that my mother had left. This bucket, the *amu*, was a marriage pot my mother had brought with her when she married. We stored our water in it since it was a special kind of pot that kept the water cool. But the *amu* held only enough water for one day. Every morning I had to put fresh water into this pot; then I had to get water to bathe myself. I had to get to school by eight, and I was always late. I did not eat anything until lunchtime. While the other students were eating, I went to the bush to search for palm kernels that had fallen from a tree. I used a stone to open the kernel to get the nuts. My lunch consisted of these palm nuts and water. I finished school by two and went straight to the farm. I ate the coco yam[22] my father had prepared and then I collected firewood for the house. Afterward, it was time to cook dinner. My father never spent money for "processed" foods such as palm oil.[23] We had all we needed on the farm, but it had to be "processed." I did this all myself. Usually I brought the palm kernels home from the farm on Saturdays. I cooked the kernels to remove the skin and pounded and squeezed them to get the oil. I made enough to last a week. When my father realized that all this work was too much for me, he asked a neighbor to cook for him; I was to cook for myself.[24] Every day, I collected the food she prepared for my father. She cooked for him for two years, but then they had a disagreement. He believed the woman was using his food to feed her four children. I began to cook for him again and continued to do so until I finished primary grade six.

My brother, Joseph Ọlabọde, and I never fought. My father hired a woman to cook for, bathe, and care for my brother. Even when I was old enough to cook for my father, the woman continued to cook for my brother. As I was cooking my food, my brother would bring his food from the woman and share it with me. When I finished cooking, I shared my food with him.

Whenever our father killed animals in the forest, he gave us the head. We cut the head: the senior child got the bottom part, which was smaller, and which included the jaw. The junior child received the top of the head, which included the brain. Younger children liked to eat the brain because it was very soft. I always liked the brain, even as I got older. I remember telling my brother one day that I liked the brain. He said that I could take it, but I told him if I did he might think that I was his junior. He said that he would not think that way and that he preferred the jaw anyway. He offered to share the brain every time from then on. The brain resembled *egusi* (melon seed), another dish I liked very much. Eventually, I began to cook for my brother, as well as for my father.

My father's mother had seven orange trees. The trees were very bountiful. One orange tree gave two sacks of oranges. When she died, she left the trees to one of her daughters, who was married and living in Ilorin. My father agreed to care for the trees since he was in Ogidi. If my brother and I were hungry while we were at the farm, we would pluck some oranges to eat. We never let our father know, though, because he would beat us with a fan belt or he would knock us so hard on the head that it felt like he'd knocked a hole in it.

We had one room and one mat. We had no bed, but we used mud to make one section of the room higher than the other and roomy enough for a large body. My father slept there, and my brother and I used the mat. When my brother and I began growing up, I asked my father for my own room. It was not a real room, only the passageway, but I began sleeping there, in my "room," anyway.

My friends and I did fun things like play hide-and-seek. The girls hid, and the boys looked for them. When they found the girls, the boys held them and pulled the girls close to them. Every evening when the moon was out, all of the girls who were of marrying age sang, "Come and put your cloth down. Let me see how naked you are." They called a girl's name and began to sing about her. They would sing, "Oh, you are beautiful in your nakedness, but we think you are not cut." They knew you were not cut because everything would be hanging out.

When they chose a girl who was circumcised, they sang, "Your nakedness is beautiful because nothing is sticking out."

All the girls used to go to the farm and look for henna. We decorated our bodies with the henna. The next day our skin would be black where we put the henna. When we went to see the masquerade our bodies looked beautiful with henna or camwood [a red cosmetic derived from the local flora]. Then we put beads on our nude bodies and danced around.

I remember one masquerade that women in our village were not allowed to take part in. The masquerade abused anyone who had done something offensive in the town. That masquerade came out to the offender's neighborhood and abused the person. The offender could not come out or reply unless the offender was a man. Husbands sometimes reported their wives to the people who participated in this masquerade. When this masquerade season began, the worshipers gathered at the front of the offender's house. They said, "You are the one who has done this thing on such-and-such a day. Now is the time that we will reply to you." They told her that her head was not correct, and the woman was not permitted to say anything.[25] The masqueraders said, "Hey, you woman who does not like to work." They abused her and said, "Look at her legs, they look like those of a guinea fowl."

# 2

## No Man Will Pay Bride-Price for Me

One day when I was still living in Ajọwa, the teachers asked all the students to bring food to school for a special occasion. The teachers gave us rice and meat. This is the best of everything, I thought to myself. But then a boy said, "Give me some of your rice." I said no and told him that everybody had his or her own share. He threatened me: "I will beat you today." On our way home he said, "Monica, I told you to give me some of your rice. You refused." "You eat your own," I said. "You have no right to mine." Then he tripped me. I fell forward and hit my leg on a stone. I could not tell everyone at home that somebody had beat me, though. When a boy makes a girl fall down, adults call the girl lazy unless she beats him back. Adults like a girl who can fight.

At first the sore from my fall was little. Three days later, though, my leg began to swell. Fluid had built up around the wound and it hurt terribly. I pressed the fluid out and cut bitter leaf to cover the sore with.* If I did not cover it, flies would follow me around, attracted by

---

*Veronia amygdalina is a shrub that grows in abundance near streams. The leaves are sold in the market. The Yorubas rub their bodies with these leaves to alleviate itching and parasitic skin diseases (Dalziel 1937/1955).

the sore and infecting it. I didn't cover the sore with a rag because I didn't want any adults to see that I had a sore. The infection got worse. My school uniform was long, so I hid it with that. I told whoever asked that the wound was healing because I was afraid that they would put something on it that would cause it to hurt more. It was not until my father came to take me from his brother's house that I received medical treatment.

My father asked me what was wrong. I told him that I had fallen down. He told me he would teach me a lesson that would stop me from hiding sores. He gave me alum. Alum is something we used to clean the water. When alum is thrown on dirty water, the dirt settles at the bottom. My father gave me some to blend with pepper.* He said that he was supposed to apply plain pepper, but mixing it with alum was suppose to lessen the pain. I cried for hours each time the medicine was applied. After the pain stopped, fluid gushed from the wound. We did this every day, but it didn't help. At least the dressing was changed regularly.

Eventually, my father took me to the hospital to get an injection. I was told to return for daily treatment, but we had no money. For three years, I had no bandage to cover the sore, so I used dirty rags. At school some of the students must have told the teacher that I had a sore. One day the teacher said, "Something smells. Everybody with sores come out here." There were three of us. Mine was the worst. "What is this?" he said. I told him that it was a little sore. He told me to uncover it. He couldn't believe all the pus coming from it. I hadn't treated it for three days. I had nothing to put on it more than an herbal poultice I made. He looked at it. Then he took his cane and beat the sore. I begged him to stop. "This will teach you a lesson," he said. He told me not to return to school until the sore was healed.

The teacher liked me. I was good in school and always made top grades. He praised me for my work but told me that I did not look after myself. He did not see the private part of my life. He did not know about all the housework I had to do. All he saw was that my father had two children. He thought my father should be able to look after us, but he did not know my father's circumstances.

The next day, my father came home from the farm very early. He

---

*Pepper is commonly used to kill germs. The Yoruba believe that germs and worms do not like the taste of pepper and should ideally be killed by it or at least run away from the pepper (Buckley 1985).

was surprised to find me there. I told him that the teacher had sent me home because of the sore. My father said he was not going to do anything for it since he already had given me 50 kobo to go to the hospital. I repeated that I could not go back to school, but he told me that was not his business. I began to work for local contractors, carrying concrete on my head, until I had enough money to go to the hospital for an injection. I went to the hospital every day and paid 3 kobo for the treatment. The sore took another six months to heal.

My father never had any money. He was a poor farmer. He also made marriage baskets, but they only brought in about 3 kobo apiece. Sometimes I had to leave school for four weeks at a time to work and earn enough to pay my school fees. The woman who cooked for my father used to help me to make a sack of *gari* to sell. I had to peel and grate the cassava, squeeze the water from it, and then fry it. A sack of *gari* weighed more than 150 kilograms and only brought in 12 shillings. My school fees were 15 shillings per trimester.

I could not afford to buy school uniforms; I had to sell firewood to earn money. The first uniform I had I used for four years, and I had only one pair of underwear. Eventually, the uniform began to tear, and I was ashamed. I asked my uncle to sell me cloth on credit. I told him I would repay him with the money my mother had contributed to a pool with her friends. Their custom was to contribute money to a pool; then each person had a turn when they could withdraw a certain amount.* I went to my mother's friend, who gave me 1 naira and 50 kobo. I bought cloth for uniforms for my brother and myself. I repaid my uncle a few kobo at a time. That is how I managed to buy a uniform two times in seven years. I wore that uniform every day, and within one year it was worn out from washing. I could not even afford to buy soda, the cheapest soap available then, to wash my uniform.

One girl noticed that I always went to the farm with a wrapper and no blouse. Her family was not poor, and they gave me a dress. My father told me to return it. I told him that I hadn't asked for it, but that this girl, Suzanne, was grateful to me because I tutored her. She was dull in school and she loved me because I helped her. I was ashamed to return the dress after accepting it, but I did not want my father to scold me, so I returned it after all.

---

*For a discussion of *esusu*, a common mutual aid association, see Fadipẹ 1970, p. 256.

One Christmas my father wanted to do something special for us. He went hunting and came back with some "bushmeat." My brother put the meat in the kitchen. I would never have done that because the kitchen was just a grass house with no door. Any dog could wander in and eat the meat, and unfortunately that is what happened. I knew if my father found out he would beat my brother. On three or four occasions my father had beaten me to the extent that my whole body was sore. I did not want my brother to get in trouble. I had about 1 shilling, or 10 kobo, saved from when I had worked carrying concrete. I went to the place where bushmeat was sold. Six pieces cost 33 shillings which was about 30 kobo. I had enough for two pieces, which I bought and put in my father's soup. He asked why he received so little, and I told him that friends had come to celebrate and had eaten some and that we had eaten the rest. But we had not eaten anything. I did not like lying, but I did not want my brother to get beaten.

My friend Angelina and I used to help each other. I sometimes helped her fetch firewood. Once she helped me to pick melon seed. It was only fair that she be given some, but I could not do it without asking my father. She insisted that I did not have to consult him. Since I had put all the seed in the house, he knew how much was there. I removed some to give to my friend. I started cooking and forgot to tell him about my friend's request. He accused me of stealing and refused to consult my friend. He said he would teach me a lesson, then started beating me. He called my brother to say that I had become a thief. I showed my body to my friend and she became upset.

Hunters frequently burn the bush looking for bushmeat. They don't care what they burn—houses, people, telephone lines. They only care about their own income. Once, when I was in primary grade five, my father's farm was burned in this way. He was devastated but grateful that we were all still alive. But when he was upset, he would yell and call me "the one who is going to die in the bush." It was like calling me stupid. It means that someone has died in another town not her hometown and none of her relatives are there to bury her.*

It upset my father that my mother was no longer alive and that I was getting older and would leave him. Then he would have no one to cook

---

*Given the centrality of ancestor worship and commemoration, not to have certain rites carried out immediately after death and regularly thereafter is the worst of all possible fates. "May you die in the bush" is an imprecation (Stone 1899).

for him. He loved me when I was a child, but he did not care for me the way a father should. He did not love my brother, Joseph, very much either. When Joseph finished his training as a tailor, my father was supposed to bring food to the celebration. He never turned up. It made Joseph so mad that he said if he ever had money he would never share it with him. People there asked where our relatives were. No one from my father's or mother's families attended. None of these people ever even gave me *gari* to drink. *Gari* is poor people's food. None of my mother's sisters cared for us. None of them ever said, "Well, she is walking naked; now take a blouse." One sister who was close to my mother once loaned me 1 cent. All I owe her is 1 kobo, 1 cent. Now she says, "I owe too much money; please come and pay. I want your best handwoven cloth. I want *adire*. I want batik."

I finished primary school in 1965. I wanted to go to secondary school, and I passed the examination, but I had no money. The deposit alone was 5 pounds, or about 10 naira. My father told me that since I had finished school, I should go and work with the bricklayers, carrying concrete on my head. There were men who cut the stone from the mountain. Others, mostly women and those who had left school and were otherwise unemployed, carried the brick to the place where the foundation for the house was being laid. It took a week to carry this stone, and the workers received so little money. For carrying about 200 stones, each one a distance of 2 kilometers, I earned about 25 kobo a week.

I told my father that my mother and great-grandmother had worked with *adire* and that I wanted to do it too. I didn't have money for the starch, though. He allowed me to use his cassava to make starch. Some students worked as altar boys with the priest of our school. I told one of the altar boys, Timothy, that I did *adire* and that I wanted the leftover candles from the mass to use as light so that I could work at night. My father told me to go show the first piece I made to the priest in Ogidi. I sold the second one I made to a woman who was related to my father. In general, I only did that work irregularly. I still cooked for my father in the evening. When cassava was out of season, I was idle the rest of the day. I had my own farm, but it made no money. Among my father, my brother, and me, we did not have 10 kobo in the house. I asked Timothy if he knew anybody in Kabba who needed someone as a laborer or nanny. I did not want to carry bricks on my head for 25 kobo a week.

One day Timothy came to see me with the priest. He said that there was an Indian woman in Kabba looking for a baby-sitter. He asked me if I had clothes because the woman didn't want anybody without dresses. I said I had two: A woman I used to help with cooking and cleaning gave me one gown. I bought two yards of cloth with the money I earned selling bottles I found—four bottles, each of which sold for 10 kobo. I fetched two loads of firewood for the tailor in exchange for her services. That is how I had two dresses. I only had one pair of underpants. When I bathed, I washed them and wore them cold and wet.

Some time after my mother's death, my mother's sisters divided her property.[1] She had fourteen wrappers and blouses. Six were good, for Sunday use. The rest were for working on the farm. The cloth she used to work on the farm was handwoven; she had made it herself. Her sisters chose the good clothes. Everything else was torn in the middle. I got one handwoven outfit and one of faded *adirẹ*. I asked them what could I take for my brother. They gave him one wrapper but no *buba* [blouse]. Women considered valuable a good chair, plates, cups, spoons, bowls. My mother had these, but I never saw any of them. Among her things I saw a plastic bucket my mother had bought when plastic became fashionable in Nigeria. I told my mother's siblings that I wanted the bucket. My mother's youngest sister said she wanted it too. I said again, "I want it," but they said, "You can't have it. You are too young. You are not going to marry. What are you going to do with it?" We argued back and forth. I told them I was going to secondary school and that I could use it then, but they let my mother's sister have the bucket. Later, when I got the job in Kabba, I asked my brother to go with me to see that sister. I told her I needed the bucket. We told her that if she did not give it to us we were going to make trouble and die on her doorsill. She told me to take the bucket and go and not to speak to her anymore.

I told my father that I was going to the job in Kabba, that if I worked, maybe I could save some money and go to secondary school. All my father wanted, though, was for me to get married so he could use my bride-price to pay for my brother's wife. I told him not to wait for my bride-price—I might not even let my husband pay anything. I was so upset; my father had made no plans for me.

At the age of sixteen, I went to work for the woman in Kabba. In the morning I bathed and went to work. In the afternoon, my employers would tell me I smelled and that I should go and wash. I only had two dresses, and I had to change twice a day. The woman offered me a place to stay in her boy's quarters, but my aunt said that I should live with her. Living with my aunt meant that I had to walk 2 kilometers to work every day. I tried to live that way for three months, but it didn't work, so I moved into the woman's boy's quarters.

I cleaned her house and looked after her four children. She paid me 2 naira and 75 kobo a month. When she went to work at eight, I took care of the baby. Indian children had to be cared for differently than Nigerian children. You couldn't put the baby on your back. The woman made me an overdress so that when the baby spat up I could change just my overgown.

I received 2 kobo a day for food, but it was not enough to buy yam. Most days I would just drink *gari* and eat palm kernels. Anytime the woman killed a chicken I was on top of the world. I ate the head and the leg.

The first time I got paid, my mother's sister wanted to borrow my pay. I told her I needed the money for dresses. She said that she owed someone money and that I had to loan it to her.

My two dresses began to get holes in them. The woman asked what had happened to my clothes. I told her I had none and that she would not have employed me if she had known. She asked me where my mother was. I told her she was dead. "I will be your mother," she said. She used my salary for that month to buy me more dresses. I was so happy because that meant I could then change four times a week.

The first slippers I bought cost 40 kobo. I only wore them when I went out with the family. Every weekend they traveled. I was so happy just to sit on the back seat. They took me everywhere—to Benin, to Lagos, to Igboland—anywhere their Indian friends lived. They took me along to watch the children. Those children were rude. They would say, "Monica, go and bathe; you smell." I would say okay. They would say, "Monica, you are oogabooga." I wouldn't say anything. One child would always say, "I don't like you. I hate you." I never said anything. I just smiled.

The woman was impressed with the way I talked to her children. She said she was going to travel to India and asked me to look after them while she was gone. She took the small baby with her, and the other children remained with her husband. She told me to pray to the Virgin Mary for her children. Every day while she was gone, I went to the picture of the Virgin Mary and said, "Mary, mother of Jesus, look after these children; don't let them get sick." When the woman came back, she was happy.

When I got my period for the first time, I was so scared I thought I was going to die.[2] No one ever told me that a woman had a period. When it first came, I went and I washed and it went away; then it came again. I did not know who to tell. I only had one pair of underpants, so the blood just spread onto my dress and my leg. I wanted to go and change, but the Indian woman had come home for lunch and the baby was still awake. I told her I wanted to go the toilet. She looked at me and said, "Monica, what is this? What is all this on your leg?" I said, "I don't know. I am sorry. It happened just a half hour ago." She asked if I had cut my leg. I said no. She asked me if I had my period and I said no. She asked me where the blood had come from. I said it was from my bottom. She explained to me that I had gotten my period. She did not have sanitary pads, so she gave me some old cloth. She showed me how to fold the cloth inside my underwear. She told me to wash the cloth after wearing it and to hang it to dry in a secluded place. I asked if I had to wash it with soap. She gave me a whole sari—six yards of cloth. I washed one piece of cloth and left it in my room. I went to tell her that one piece of cloth was wet and the other one was dirty. She told me to cut the whole sari into pieces.

She explained to me that I was having a period. She said things like, "Don't sleep with a man because he will only want to have intercourse with you. Now that you have a period, he can have sex with you and you will become pregnant." She asked me if any man had ever fondled me. I said no. She said that if a man had intercourse with me now, it would spoil my life. After that I would just yell at any man who wanted to fondle me. I would scream and shout to keep him away.

One night I dreamed that my aunt who lived in Kabba wanted to give me *moinoin* [steamed bean paste] to eat. I said, "Why should I take *moinoin*? That is how they poisoned my mother, and she died. I am not taking it." When I woke up I decided to ask my aunt to repay the 1 pound she had borrowed from me. When I arrived at her house, I found out that she was pregnant. I told her I needed the money because I had to loan it to my father. I had no money at all. She told me that she had no money but that I could take her jewelry and sell it. Anything I made over 1 pound should be returned to her. I looked at her condition and I thought to myself, "This woman is going to have a baby and she asked me to take her jewelry." I blamed myself for asking her for the money. When I left her I cried. Here, we think about the possibility of the baby dying at birth. I was afraid that if my aunt had the baby and it died, she would blame me because she would have worried about the delivery day and about repaying me. I prayed that she would have a safe delivery.

One month later, my aunt gave birth to twins; they both died at birth. I was so upset about asking her about the money.

My father came to me one day and asked for all of my salary. I said, "Salary! The first month, my mother's sister took it. The second month, the woman bought dresses for me. The money I saved from my food, I used to buy slippers." My father said he came because his dead wife's sister (my aunt) received 2 naira and he never got anything. He said that he was the one who had paid for my school fees. I told him that he never had money and that I worked to put myself through school. I know I used his cassava and lived in his house, but before I could get anything for myself I had to work. I cut the cloth that I inherited from my mother into two. I used one as a wrapper and the other to cover myself at night. I was trying to save money to buy more dresses for myself. Whenever my brother came to visit I gave him a gown because he was wearing a torn shirt. He was dressed like a girl even though he was a boy.

When I did not give my father the money he said to me, "There is a civil servant that I want you to marry. He has a cocoa business." I looked at myself. My breasts had just begun to develop. My father told me the man wanted me to train to become a policewoman. If I did not want to be a police officer, he would make me a secretary. I did not want to become a secretary either.

I couldn't tell my employer that my father wanted me to leave. He told me that if I did not agree to marry the man, he would make me suffer more than I already had. I told myself that if that was the case, he would never see me again. I used to make up songs in my head: "This world, this world. You have to be afraid of people in this world." When my mother died, I stopped trusting people. If my mother had been alive I wouldn't have had all this suffering. My mother was a hard-working woman. Even after her death, people said, "What a woman!" Here they say a mother is the gold treasure. She cares about your life and worries if you are not okay.

The full saying is mothers are like gold and fathers are like glass.

The men in our village married for business, not for love. They married to make life easier for themselves. They wanted somebody to look after them. All they wanted was to sell their daughters in marriage to get the bride-price. And their sons were put on the farms to make food for them. The men would relax and become "fathers with many children." They just waited for the end of their lives, when they expected their children to kill cows and buy cloth to bury them. They never helped their children to get ahead in life.

My mother never wanted to marry my father. She wanted to marry someone who drove a taxi because he would earn more and be better educated than a farmer. My father always hated us for that, and he made us suffer for it. But in general, fathers always preferred sons to daughters. Sons kept the father's name going. That is why my father wanted to have another baby after me. He said that if he had a boy, his name would never die.

There is an exception. If a man loved his wife it showed on her children. If a child from a wife a man does not like dies, he tells the favored child from the favored wife not to worry because she or he is worth one hundred children to him. But the mother of the dead child will never have another one to take that child's place. A father feels bad enough to kill himself when anything bad happens to the favored child.

When I was young, my father was nice to me. He cooked food at the farm and brought it to my brother and me. He made sure there was kerosene for the lamp so we didn't have to sleep in the dark. Though he had no money for cloth, he made sure we had a mat to sleep on. As I grew older, he saw me becoming more independent and he began to make me feel bad for being a girl. He said that girls were useless. Men only made them pregnant and then they moved to their husbands' houses. Girls never kept their fathers' names going. Now my father is proud of me because he sees that a woman can do what a man can do.

My father had his own vision that I would become pregnant by the first man who came along. Knowing that he believed this, I did not want it to become true for me. If it did, I would be useless and nothing more than a housewife. I worked hard to be what I wanted to be. I did not want to hear my father say, "I knew you would be nothing."

The last time my father came to visit me, I told him I wanted to buy a piece of land, where my students would have room and I would be able to do what I want to do. He asked me to take him to the land.

When we arrived, I told him that the land was owned by a man who was more important than me; he had finished university. I reminded my father that he did not send me to secondary school or to university, that all he ever said was that a girl was useless. Many years ago he had told me plainly that all he wanted was to get a dowry from me so he could pay for a wife for my brother. Until this day, he has never received anything from a man for me. Now, if my brother wants to marry, I can pay the bride-price from my own pocket. But I made sure my father never got a bride-price for me.

All men want when they have a daughter is to sell her to a man, who in turn uses her like a slave. The husband only pays 50 naira for the wife, an amount that does not even pay for what the girl's parents have contributed to her upbringing. Yet this 50 naira gives the man rights to the woman for life. I never wanted any man to claim his right to me through a bride-price. If a man never pays a bride-price for me, I can always be free to move and be independent. If he pays a bride-price he can force me to do many things; he can say, "I have paid your bride-price; I can do anything I want to you." He can take your children or he can force you out of your home.

# 3

-----

# I Went to Learn
# about Life

It happened that at the same time my father was arranging my marriage, my friend Justina approached me with an interesting proposition. She told me that a man from our village had started a traveling theater group. He said that people who wanted to join his group should follow any theater company that came to Kabba. Then they should send word to him, and he would come and get them. When she was through with her story, I began to tell her about my problems. I didn't want to marry this minister at all. He was forty and already had several wives. When I was a child my family lived in his house. Whenever he saw me he would say, "You are growing." Instead of consenting to this marriage, I thought, I could just leave with my friend and join the theater.[1] Justina said that there was a theater group playing that night at St. Augustine's College, a local junior high school. She suggested that we go and watch. We decided to join the theater. Justina believed that since no one was with the theater in Ogidi other than this one man from our village, our relatives would send him to look for us.

That afternoon, I told the woman I was working for that I was going to get something to eat. I sent for one of my friends to go and work in my place. I told her to tell my boss that my father wanted me to go and join the police force. In fact, my father waited for me along the road

27

that led to Ogidi until evening. He had come to take me to the minister. Justina and I took the road that led to where the theater would be performing that night. That is how I left. The man who was in charge of that theater group was named Olusunta. We left with the group that night and began to travel to nearby towns. We began to make money.

The minister wondered where I had gone. His daughter told him that she had seen the Indian woman's baby-sitter watching the theater at her school. The minister sent my father to find us. My father made a statement to the local police that Olusunta had stolen me.

Eventually they found us. The police came to arrest the group. They charged the group with kidnapping the minister's brother's daughter.* The police wanted to put them in jail, but the members asked if they could just release us from their group. The police agreed. They took us to the police station, where my father was waiting. The police asked me if I knew him. I said he was my father, but Justina said that she did not know my father at all, so the police told him that he could only take me. As soon as the lorry stopped in Ogidi, Justina's family asked where she was. They were happy to hear that they might get her back later.

My father took me to Kabba, where the minister lived. The minister was so happy to have me back. Then my father left to return to Ogidi. The minister looked at me and said, "Well, you are getting tall. How old are you now?" "Sixteen," I said. In another three years I would be just right, he said. Then he measured my breasts. He said, "You are thirty-two and a half. You are small, but that is okay. I will look after you." I knew this man was looking for a wife.

The minister told me he would keep me as his secretary. He said that based on the measurement of my breasts I would not be able to train as a police officer, since a woman's breast size had to be at least thirty-four to do so. I only had a primary school education and could not write very well. He said that he would place me with a secretary who would train me. He had plans to take me to Benin City the next day and arranged for me to stay in a room at one of his houses. All of my clothes were with the theater group, however, so I asked the minister if I could go and get them. He said I could and asked me to bring Justina back with me. He offered me money, but I told him I had

---

*People from the same village refer to each other as brother and sister though they may not be related by blood. This fact probably stems from the cultural idea that the king was the father or progenitor of his people (Johnson 1921/1966).

enough for the trip. He said he hoped that I was not going to run away again.

Around four that evening, I went to the garage to find public transportation. I had only had 10 kobo with me. The theater group had given it to me for food and good luck and had asked me to return to them if their group survived. I told them I would, and Justina told me that she would check daily at the motorpark to see whether or not I had arrived in case I did not have enough money to pay for my transportation.

To go from Kabba to the next stop, where I would get on another vehicle to take me halfway to Ikarę, which was where the theater group was, cost 15 kobo. To travel from that point to Ikarę required another 15 kobo. When we arrived at the first stop the driver asked me for payment. I told him that someone was meeting me in the next town and that if he could arrange for me to get a driver to take me there, the person meeting me would give the money to the second driver, who would send it back to the first. The driver agreed.

At Ikarę, the theater group was waiting. Justina paid the driver. At first, I urged her to return with me to Ogidi. People there were saying that I was the one who made her run away, I told her. But she said that she was not going back. We began talking about my problems. I told her that I did not want to marry that minister. I would have been wife number ten. My father was poor and I was poor, so if I married that man, his other wives would have just used me as their slave. In fact, my father's real plan for me was to give me to the minister as a gift. The man had no love for me; he just liked me because I was young. He was going to do anything he liked to me. Justina convinced me not to go back.

Olusunta, who had a wife and two other women who lived with them, had founded his theater group about seven years before I joined. The group used posters to advertise their performances. If the group performed and made money, we each received 2 or 3 kobo. There were sometimes periods of five days, though, where we made no money. Whenever this happened, we walked to the next town, carrying all of our belongings.

Anytime we went to a new town, I worked carrying concrete on my head. I made 3 kobo a day and used that money for food. There was no money for soap, however. My hair became infested with lice, so I shaved it off. We used my bald head in a comedy act. I would make funny faces to the audience, then bow and take off my cap. The audience thought that I was a man and were amused to discover that I was a woman. Justina could not act or sing, so she just opened the curtain.

In general, the performance began with an opening glee, or prayer for the protection of the audience, that their enemies would not kill them. The director usually performed this and would then introduce the play while I described with my hands what was going to happen. We sang a little song that said that nobody should insult us because we have all had our baths. Then someone recited a proverb. There were about six of us who could sing. We all dressed alike. We bought bright-colored clothes from secondhand stores. Those who had a bit of money made their own costumes. We danced to the rhythm of the drums. Often we performed plays about enmity among co-wives. The story went something like this: The junior wife poisoned the food of the senior wife's child. For killing the child, the woman was banished to "the bush of ghosts." It was expected that the ghosts would eat the guilty person. The guilty woman cried and told of her suffering, but she was still banished.

Our performances lasted about two hours, and we charged from 5 to 10 kobo for admission. We only played in small towns because the larger ones had many theater groups, and we could not afford to pay for the halls in the big towns. It cost up to 50 naira to rent a hall in a big town, but in a small town the rent was only 1 or 2 naira.

Not many women were in the theater. Most of the leaders were men. I had an idea that if I had the chance I would like to be the leader of a group. I wanted people to say, "She really tried," which means I did very well. Anyone who so desired could found their own theater. All they needed to do was to provide the costumes and make up the acts and plays. Generally, directors recruited people by telling them they would be well paid. People who were unemployed were especially attracted by the directors' offers. But they did not know that once they joined, they would be strung along. The director constantly told the members that the next month they would be better off. The next month would come, and they would be no better. The directors had silver tongues.

As the youngest member of the group, I did most of the work. The younger members had to wash the bosses' clothes and costumes and fetch water for drinking and bathing for all the members. After traveling around with the group and working this way for some time, I just began to cry. "My father wanted to marry me off to a rich man, and I refused," I said. "Now I am suffering. I want to go home." The director said, "Your father has made you go crazy." My head felt like it was going to crack. I told Justina that I was leaving, but she urged me not to. She said that although we were suffering now, things would be better in the future.

Later on, Justina warned me that one of the men in the theater group was going to marry her and that they were going to use me for black magic to get money, or, as the saying went, "Somebody was going to carry a calabash." When my name was called, then, money would come out of the calabash, or gourd. To do this, they were going to take me to an herbalist. But it meant that I would be dead. I would be killed in the ritual.[2] When I heard their plans, I was terrified. I started thinking: I have only one brother; who would take care of him? If I died, no one in my village would know where or how I died. I prayed that someone would come and get me.

Our relatives had been looking for us for three weeks; they felt that it would be a disgrace to the village to lose two girls who belonged to royal families.* They contacted the man from our village who had his own theater group. His was the only theater group that went to Ogidi, since our village was so small. They promised to give the man anything he wanted if he could find us, so he arranged to charge them a fee. He began to look for us through our troupe's posters and traced us through a number of towns to where we were performing.

I was out fetching water when the man arrived. He told Olusunta that the government had sent him and that he was to give financial assistance to small theater companies that demonstrated promise. He had heard, he said, that the company was good, so he tracked them down. The company was very happy and proud. The man asked them if the entire group was assembled before him. They told him no, that two girls were not present. He asked them where they had found us two girls, and they replied that we were from Kabba. The man gave them 2 naira and told them to perform their play while he watched. If they were good, the man told them, they would get a grant to go to the United States.

The members of the group did not suspect him of mischief because he had facial marks from the Yoruba (that is, from Ibadan, which was

---

*See chapter 1.

in Ọyọ State), not from Kwara State, which would have linked him to
Ogidi.* So they expected him to help them. The man waited half an
hour for us to come back. Then he told the group that he wanted to buy
a newspaper. He asked a woman in the town where people went to get
water. She described the road to him and he went to look for us. When
he saw us, he asked me if I was the daughter of Ojo. Our relatives had
given him our photographs. I did not recognize him. He turned to
Justina and told her that she was the niece of Elega.† Justina recog-
nized him as the man who was looking for theater members for his
group when he was in Ogidi.

I wanted to go back to my village with him. My heart had already
left the group. Justina did not want to leave. I felt that if we went back,
people would be relieved to know that we were well. I urged her to let
the man have the glory of returning us since he took the trouble to find
us. When we went back to the group, the man told Olusunta and the
others that he really came to take us back to our village. They refused
to let us go because, they said, we caused them a lot of problems and
they felt they had invested their energy in us. Then the man insisted
that we go with him because we were his sisters.

The theater members disputed our relatedness because he had tribal
marks from the Yoruba people in Ibadan in Ọyọ State and we were
from Kwara State. The man spoke to us in our Ogidi dialect and I
answered him. They asked me if I knew him. I said that I was the
last-born of his father, but Olusunta still would not let us go.

We all went to the police station to try to resolve this. The man had
a motorcycle and arrived at the police station before the rest of us. He
made his statement and gave the police 10 shillings. When Olusunta
arrived and gave the police his statement, they told him he was wrong.
The police gave the man the authority to take us away.

I asked the man to take us back to Ogidi. He felt, however, that if he
took us back to our village, people would find out that he was the one

---

*The "ila," or pattern of facial marks a person bears, is a function of one's class
position (e.g., being from the nobility) and membership in one of the many sub-
groups which collectively comprise the Yoruba-speaking people. The city, Ibadan,
includes a vast number of Ọyọ-Yorubas. This man's marks attest to his membership in the Ọyọ-Yoruba group. Ọyọ-Yorubas share a distinct cultural and linguistic
heritage which distinguishes them from the Yagba, Ijumu, Ikiri, Abinu, and Igbede
peoples of the Kabba-Yoruba region, Davies's homeland.

†"Elega" cannot be identified.

who put it into our minds to run away to join the theater in the first place. Instead, he took us to Oṣogbo. He wanted to produce his own play. He included us as members of his theater group. Once in Oṣogbo, we did his bidding. If he said sing, we sang. If he told us to dance, we danced. He was pleased with us and wanted to keep us in Oṣogbo. He had wanted to sleep with Justina from the first night we arrived. Justina and I slept together on the floor that first night. The next morning Justina asked, "My friend, do you know what happened last night?" I said no. She said, "You slept away; you sleep like a baby. This man came to me in the night. He was playing with my breasts. He was wearing a chain around his neck and I pulled it." The second morning the man took Justina to the Oṣun shrine to fetch water. He showed her around. He took her into one of the small buildings, laid her down, and tried to rape her. She said she started screaming to the passers-by to come and get her. He asked her how she could be so "bush." He did not believe that she had never been with another man. Even if she had, she told him, men do not just rape women. Justina did not want to sleep with him because he was married already. Besides, she did not even want to marry anyone from Ogidi.

One day I embroidered a palm tree with a naked figure underneath it. My work caught the man's attention. He asked me if I knew how to do other things. I said yes, I could do *adire*, but I had been doing only embroidery recently. In Ogidi I sold my work for 5 to 10 kobo each. I sold some pieces to my friend's sister, who was a tailor. Sometimes the tailor, Regina, would give me work to do: stitching a flower on a pillowcase, for instance. I also made bedspreads, for which the tailor gave me the cloth and thread. So the man liked my work. I told him that I had learned to embroider in school. My relatives gave me an embroidered piece that my mother made, and I love it so much. Eventually I decided to make my own patterns and added trees and birds. The man said he would buy a piece from me for 50 kobo, but he never gave me the money. He gave me cloth to make *adire* shirts for his band members. Then he gave me a pen, some ink, and a design, which I copied exactly. He really liked my work. He said that even if he took me back to Ogidi, he would like for me to come back and work for him. I agreed, but I still wanted to go home. I told him that he would not get any glory if Justina and I were not returned home. I was willing to work for him, but only after relieving my relatives of their worries.

One month later he took us home. He hired a taxi to take us there directly. I wanted him to take us back on a Sunday, when everyone would be at home, at around noon, when everyone would be back from church, sitting around and doing nothing. People usually went to their farms on weekdays. When we arrived in Ogidi, I asked the driver to move slowly through the village. I shouted, "You people in Ogidi, this man brought your daughters back. You better look at us." Everyone came running, because it was rumored that we were lost.

Before I left Ogidi I was shy and never talked much. The theater opened my eyes. People wondered how this quiet girl could have run away to the theater. When a crowd of about fifty had gathered, I said, "Now I am going to make a speech." Everyone was silent. "You people who think I got lost are wrong. I only went to learn about life. I suffered more than before I left home, and I never knew when I was going to stop suffering." Then I said, "I am going to sing for you." I sang and made faces. Then I explained, "Those are just a few things that I learned in the theater. I am somebody you will be talking about in the future."

It came time for the man to turn us over to our relatives. They gave him many presents: beer, schnapps, and money. My family and Justina's family made food for him. They were so happy. They wanted to make him an important man in the village, because, by bringing us back, he was the one who prevented the village from having a bad name.

The next morning the families gathered. I told the man that he should explain in public how he had suffered to find us. The people who were gathered there asked me who caused me to run away. I told them that it was my father, because he wanted me to marry a minister. They asked Justina and me what we wanted to do with our lives. Justina's family agreed to give her money to begin trading. But my father had no money to start me in a trade or train me further. All my father could say was that he wanted me to join the police force. I told him that I would not return to his house to cook and clean for him. Instead I went to stay with my great-grandmother. She was living in Ogidi in one of our family houses. She had moved from Ajọwa when she heard that I left, and she was very sad.

One of my father's relations gave me 5 kobo. I bought and processed melon seed to sell. I fried the seeds and sold portions for 1 kobo each. I made a profit of 1 kobo. I did this for one month and managed to save 30 kobo. I planned to use that money to make batiks. Then the man wrote me a letter asking me when I would return to Oṣogbo. I was happy to receive the letter. I wanted to go back to Oṣogbo because what he was doing was similar to what I wanted to do. He told me that I was very talented and that he would introduce me to Suzanne Wenger, an Austrian woman who was helping a lot of the artists. He said that since I was ready to work hard, he knew a woman who was willing to help me. She was a woman who liked to help female artists. I was so happy. My mother had died, but now that I was ready to work, someone was ready to help me.

I was worried about the way the man was troubling Justina. My heart told me that as soon as he stopped looking at Justina, he would begin troubling me.

I did not want to tell my great-grandmother that I was leaving. I told my mother's youngest sister. Justina had gone to Kaduna to start her business; I had no one to help me. The man did not send my travel fare, so I used the 30 kobo I had made selling melon seed. It was not enough. I needed 20 kobo more.

The day I left I took a marriage basket made from palm trees that my father had made for my mother. I walked two kilometers from the village to get a taxi, because I did not want anyone to know I was leaving. The driver charged me 20 kobo for the trip to Ikarẹ. I explained to a driver in Ikarẹ that someone was waiting for me in Oṣogbo who would pay the balance when we arrived.

The same day I returned to Oṣogbo, the man was going to Ilọrin. He put me in the car. On the way back, he tried to force me to have sex with him. I screamed, "I haven't done it before and I have never seen such a big prick in my life! What do you want to do?" "Just wait," he said. He grabbed me and I started to scream. People outside were screaming, "Open the door." He said, "Somebody is going to eat the soup; you don't need to rush it. I'm going to eat your soup. Go and write it down."*

Once I got settled in Oṣogbo, I slept in the man's living room on a mat that I picked up and put away in the morning. I had to earn the money to buy the mat; he did not provide it. I was often sent to buy soft drinks and, as the vendors were not taking the bottles back at that time, I sold them and used the money to buy a mat. The women newcomers all slept together in the living room. I also helped the man's wife with her baby.

---

*Eating is routinely associated with sexual penetration. According to Matory (1994), a young man who is sexually interested in a woman may state his desire by saying, "I am going to eat that yam!" (p. 267).

The boys who came to learn about plays or painting slept downstairs. Some of the boys were in the man's Afro-beat band.[3] They performed at funerals, naming ceremonies, and weddings. Others were dancers, artists, and drummers. There were not many girls, and they did not come to learn. The man had one bedroom; his wife, another; Wahabi, a band boy and former cook for Ulli Beier, another; and Samuel, a painter, had the fourth bedroom. The house belonged to a native of Oṣogbo. There was a big hall connected to the house, and, in total, the rent came to 4 naira a month.

Once I had to learn to play the guitar, but within a week my finger swelled because we did not have the correct equipment. Everybody always liked me because I wore trousers like the boys, I had no breasts, and I got along with them. The boys would tell me that our boss slept with any girl that came there. They wanted to marry me. I told them that I did not come there to marry. I came to work and make a name for myself, so they should forget me. Little by little they stopped talking to me; they thought I wanted to marry the boss because he had money. I wanted to keep playing music and doing what I enjoyed. People were surprised to see a woman playing a guitar onstage; later the audience started insulting me. They said, "A woman with trousers—when she has a baby she will put the baby in her pocket." I did not respond, but they kept taunting me. The band members would tell them that a member of the audience had no right to talk to me that way, but I did not care if they abused me.

I continued to dance when we traveled to Benin, Ifẹ, Ibadan, and Lagos, and performed traditional routines based on folktales, while others did acrobatics. We wore a wrapper to cover our breasts, a short wrapper as a skirt, and sometimes a heavy headdress. The singers sang the story and the dancers performed it. One dance was based on the story of a deaf girl who was always blamed for bad things that happened in the compound. There was another girl, however, who would kill a sheep or put bugs in the people's food and blame it on the deaf girl. Eventually the people in the compound took the girls on a seven-year trek across several mountains to a bird who could see and read people's futures. The bird said that the deaf girl had had enemies before she was even born. The deaf girl's enemies killed her mother and were doing these bad things and blaming them on her. The bird said that the person suspected of doing the bad things should be thrown into the red sea, but there was no red sea in the area. Instead the people went to a pool of water and told the water before each person entered: "If the person is guilty, blood should appear. The inno- cent person will go down three times, coming out clean the first and second times and wealthy the third time." The deaf girl went in three times and came out beautifully dressed the third time. The other girl went in and came out twice, but drowned the third time. The water turned red from her blood.

When the singers sang the bird's lines, the dancers moved their heads like birds. We started off slowly and then moved our necks very fast. It was not an easy job, and when I finished my whole body would hurt. I did not dance anymore after we began having a lot of guests.*

Although he promised, the man never took me to see Suzanne Wen- ger, the Austrian artist. Instead, he sketched designs and I colored them. Soon I was designing his paintings and selling his work. He took me to Lagos, where we would trek from one house to another to sell paintings. I followed him, carrying all the plywood on my head. He told me I gave him good luck and he gave me 20 naira. I earned about 30 kobo a week. I ate on only 2 or 3 kobo and then gathered some leaves that grew in the forest near our compound. I worked day and night. Some days I had to do concrete work to make enough money to eat. The other people in the compound caused a lot of problems. If anyone took *gari* out with the thought of preparing it, and left the *gari* unattended for a few minutes, others would take the food. The thief or thieves would replace the *gari* with soil and leave a little *gari* on top to initially fool the owner of the *gari*. They would go to people's farms, take cocoa yam, and steal everything. It became a place where a person either stole or did not eat. No one wanted to work.

Instead of stealing, I ground pepper for customers. At least once a week, I did the bricklayer work, for which I was paid 50 kobo a day. I worked from morning until evening. The only time I could do this work was when he traveled, though. I did all my artwork at night, seldom sleeping. Before leaving on a trip he would give me enough work for one day—or for one week. He might give me a drawing on an eight-foot-by-four-foot length of plywood, and I would have to finish it in one week whether I wanted to or not. He did not care if I slept or not. If ink spilled on the wood, he used my money to replace the spilled ink, leaving me no money from my salary to buy food.

He treated no one right—not even his wife. His first wife performed

---

*The guests were generally expatriates visiting and working in Nigeria. They came to the compound for exposure to African art forms.

in his theater. She did not design artwork right away. Initially she kept having babies. Her first child was just a year old when she got pregnant with her second one. The way her husband treated her was terrible. He told me, though, "I am not going to treat you like I treat my senior wife, because she is lazy." My heart always told me, though, that even though he might not treat me like that at first, one day I might have a junior wife [a third wife for him], and he would treat me that way.

He always treated his first wife badly. She could not work like the rest of us because she was constantly pregnant and caring for the children. I went out with her sometimes, and we were friendly with each other. Sometimes she needed money for medicine. It might be only 20 kobo, but her husband would say there was no 20 kobo to be had. He beat her sometimes to the extent of pulling her up and down the stairs. "Why do you get pregnant?" he would say. "Do I ask you to get pregnant?" I cried to myself when this happened. I asked him why he beat a pregnant woman, and he replied, "She is lazy; she doesn't want to work; she wants something for nothing. She is the one who made me have babies with other women. Because she is lazy I have to go out and look for other wives."

I was constantly afraid that this man was going to use black magic on me. He put something in my drink on the day he raped me. I became pregnant, and from that moment he was my husband. He went to my village to tell my father and to pay the bride-price.[4] My father said, "Pay for what? Not for my daughter. A dog will never catch a fish in the river." My husband would not let me return to Ogidi. He said, "This one is caught already." I believe it was black magic. When he used it, no one could get around his power. I was not able to leave him until his power was spoiled.[5] Until that time, I always told myself that I would manage; I would survive.

The next woman who became his wife was from the same village as me. When this woman, Muni [Muniratu Bello], arrived, he told me he was going to send her away. I asked him why he had made Muni pregnant if he did not want her. He replied that it was only me that he wanted. I would not let him send her away, though, so she stayed with us. As for myself, I was not jealous. I told him that Muni was not a problem and that we could all live together. He asked me if I was sure, and I told him that I was. Though I had no baby, I was living in the compound before Muni arrived. That is how Muni's child came to be senior to my own son, although she is still my junior wife.

# 4

# The King of the Poor People

Every day our husband fought with his wives. If he did not fight with me he fought with Muni or the senior wife. Neighbors frequently tried to stop the fights, but he still would not stop. Soon the neighbors said that we caused too much trouble and that we should move. They were afraid that if our husband killed one of us, the police would arrest everyone in the area.

He jumped on us, beat us, kicked us, stood on our bellies and jumped up and down, and said, "I want you to die. I want you to die." He attacked us anywhere; if he jumped on one of us outside after a rainfall, that woman would be pushed down in the mud, and her clothes would be ruined. When he beat one wife, the others asked him to stop. But if we moved to intervene he pulled our hair or our clothes and started fighting with us. When he was in that state, he did not even recognize the children. He kicked even them if they asked him to stop. We started calling him the most wicked man because he had no sympathy for women and children.

He used to abuse us by singing songs like this:*

> Before I married you, you did not want to marry me. When you started your life you did not have two cloths. You are a useless teenager. Go and bang your head. You have been married before. You never planned

*Individuals orally compose songs to praise or abuse others (Delano 1973).

39

to become more than a prostitute. Prostitutes are different. Some have children before they become a prostitute and some have no children before they become a prostitute. If you want to sell yourself, go to your father's house. Go and buy powder, eyeshadow, and lipstick. Become the chief of lipstick, then your cheek [pride] will go down and you will become a "big" madam by force.

A big madam is someone who is independent.

The wicked husband abuses the wife before the wife can abuse him back by singing. Anytime there was a fight between our husband and one of the wives, the wife was called a prostitute. Our husband would say to us, "Who will marry you? No one wants to marry a prostitute." He would say he made a mistake by marrying us. If he had known, he would not have married a prostitute. He did not want us to wear makeup. He did not want us to wear a matching wrapper and blouse. People would see us and say we wives were not tidy.

When he saw a woman for the first time, he spoke with a silver tongue about how women need to be petted.[1] That was just to draw the woman in. When the woman was finally in, she was in trouble. Finally, the neighbors told us to take our trouble and go. At first he refused to go. He told them that they were not the landlord. One neighbor replied that his son was the landlord. That is how we left our first house.

We were often chased from house to house. The first house we lived in had three rooms. One was for our husband, another was the parlor, and the third was ours. There were three of us living in the room. When he wanted to have sex with one wife, the other two had to turn their faces to the wall. We had to close our eyes. We could not move and we could not even cough. If we made a sound, he would leave the woman he was with and come over to us, pinch us, kick us, and say we were jealous.

On the day that we left the first house, the naming ceremony for our husband's friend's first child was being performed. We all lived in the same compound. The friend's wife was very young. Our husband had encouraged his friend to marry this woman while they were certain she was still a virgin. The man complained to our husband that he could not see himself marrying a twelve-and-a-half-year-old girl, but our husband talked the man into marrying this girl by saying that in a few years some other man would be having sex with her. Our husband threatened the man, saying that if his friend did not want her, he would kidnap her for himself. When the girl came to the compound, some of the men captured her. Our husband held the girl's legs. His friend complained that he had a sister and would not want anyone to treat her that way. Our husband said that if his friend did not have sex with the girl, he would do it with her himself. The man told him that he had no right to do that, and the two men started fighting. In the end, the man had sex with the girl, and she became pregnant.

Our husband became jealous when he saw them preparing the naming ceremony for that man's child, so we started packing to move. The band boys who were living in the compound with us did not agree to move. They stayed in the house to attend the naming ceremony. The following day, the band boys moved to our new house, but our husband accused them of staying with his enemy. He told them he did not want to use them anymore and started fighting with them.

We finally settled into a three-bedroom house. This house was in the woods, and it became our husband's first gallery. We had no neighbors. There was no community and no law that said you could not beat or abuse people. If he killed someone, no one would ask him any questions. He always told us that if he killed us he would be the one to win. He said he would lie to the police.

Only one old man lived nearby. Initially when he heard us being beaten, he tried to intercede. Our husband accused the old man of using witchcraft against him. One day, our husband made the man take a stone to the Ọṣun shrine. The stone was called ṣigidi.[2] The man had always worshiped this stone, as had his great-grandfather. At the shrine, our husband made the man take off his clothes. He and four of his boys beat the old man and told him to throw the stone in the river. They nearly killed him. The man went to the king of Oṣogbo to complain. The king sent for our husband, but he never went. Our husband hated the old man because he tried to stop him from beating us, but the same thing happened when we were chased from the other houses. The neighbors would try to intercede and we were thrown out.

People said that our husband was crazy. They asked us why we stayed with him. He told us that if we left him he would kill us or make us go crazy. Most of these things scared us. Many of us were without family, and we had nowhere to run for protection. Sometimes it was not possible to depend on the police; whoever could pay them the highest price would win the case.

By then, there were four wives; the junior wife slept on the balcony. Each wife had a twin-size bed. Our husband never slept with any of us overnight. He just had sex on the woman's bed and then returned to his own room. After I had four children, I learned something new about sex. We four wives were talking with another wife who had left our husband and married someone else. She told us that whenever her new husband climaxed when having sex with her, he never waited for her to "release," and that is why she never became pregnant. I was so surprised. I asked her how a woman could release. She asked me if I had ever released. I said, "No. What is that?" She said, "The moment you release you will know because in one second everything will be different." I had never felt "different." She asked me if I enjoyed sex. I said no. She explained everything and told me I was like an ordinary woman who never had any sexual experience. The way our husband had sex was to come into our room and please himself. Sex was over as soon as he climaxed. Then he was off to someone else's bed. Sometimes he would want to sleep with seven wives without washing himself. He felt that that would bind all the wives together. By having each other's wetness, we would all be one. I consented one time. It felt like fire when he did not wash himself after having sex with so many. After my first experience, I never again let him do that with me. Whenever I heard him coming, I locked my door and told him that I was okay. I did not need or want sex. For a good sixteen years, I did not really enjoy sex and did not want a man to go to bed with me. Anyway, I became pregnant too quickly. I had my work and that was enough for that time. I finally had the experience of releasing when I remarried. I did not know that if a man really loved a woman he would care about her experiences. In this marriage it was like business, like master and slave or landlord and tenant.

We always had guests. They were young girls who had left their mothers' houses. They were "street girls" who had no homes. They slept on the balcony or in any other available space. Our husband felt that they could be useful in the future. He kept them around to work for us, and little by little he would go to bed with them. He married two like that. One had a baby and went away with the child. There were so many, I don't even remember some of their names. Some stayed two years, and others stayed five years. It was like a school with so many people coming and going. He never associated with people who were important. He was the king of the poor people. He was rich and the others were poor. And he was always in control.

Once the man who promoted my husband's work abroad came to the house. He wanted to take a picture of our husband with all his wives. Our husband told us to dress up. We all put on dresses of the same cloth, and he had a matching shirt. We started making fun of ourselves. When people see us together like this, we said, with him sitting in the middle of us all, they will say, "What a happy family." We had not even eaten that day.

Whenever he had visitors, we never disappointed him. We never showed his character. We tried to hide it. Even if he was treating one of us badly, the other wives would talk to that wife and encourage her not to show that there was no unity in the family. We knew we were not happy, but we did not want to make him look small in front of his visitors.

We bought food from vendors for our children. Sometimes there was not enough food for everyone. If one of the wives had food only for her and for her children, she was not obligated to feed anyone else. Some would shut their doors and eat in private. After we began to get along better, we shared our food with one another. Anyway, in a polygamous marriage, if a woman does not share her food with the other members of the compound they say she is wicked. I never liked locking my door to feed my child. I did not believe that my children were better than the other wives' children.

When our husband traveled abroad he did not leave us money. His mother, who lived with us, had no money either. Sometimes we could not sell our work, and there was little money for food. To get money, his mother would go and greet her church members, and they would pray together. When she got ready to leave, they would give her 2 naira. Here, when someone greets you, you have to give them a little present. Our husband's mother went from one person to the next that way, and we went with her. With the money she received, we would buy bouillon cubes, dried okra, and corn cereal. Five kobo worth of okra, after we prepared it, could feed many people. Most people eat this soup with fish, but we never had any fish. This is what we had to feed the children for the whole day.

We prayed for foreigners to come and buy our artwork. The landlord was always trying to evict us. We prayed and fasted a lot. We walked about three kilometers to some big rocks, climbed up on them, and prayed for people to come.* We were only fasting because there was no food.

To make things worse, our husband did not often allow us to go out. When we did go out, we had to return by six o'clock in the evening. At six o'clock, our husband put a guard at the door and gave him the keys. Because we so often bought food outside the compound for dinner, we had to leave the compound after six. Even though we wanted to send the two young wives to buy the food, we knew our husband would think they had gone out to see men. He would punish them and would not believe that we were the ones who sent them out. We decided that it would be best for all of us to go out together. We all went—even the pregnant ones. Once, I was pregnant, and so were Muni and the sixth wife. The sixth wife was good at jumping over the compound wall. Muni and I were the lazy ones. We couldn't jump over anything. Muni used her hands to push me over, and I would often fall on my back or scratch my feet. The wall was taller than any of us. We went over the back wall to go out, but coming back in was another problem. We had to lift ourselves up over the wall. The people who could lift themselves were the last ones to go over; they helped the rest of us first.

Our husband told the guard to kill any of the wives that tried to go out without permission. One time, one of the wives wanted to travel to her village. The guard told her that she could not go because our husband did not give her permission. She told him to go to hell. He started to beat her. We all went outside and told him, "Once you beat one, you will try to beat us all. You are a guard, not our husband." The guard said that we were right but that his boss had given him instructions to keep us in line. He said that the wife he had beaten would be our lesson. The woman got hold of the wire he had used to beat her. He managed to get her on the ground, and then he took out a very sharp Hausa knife. He cut her hands, and blood began to rush from them. We took her to the police station. The police came to arrest the guard, but he refused to go. The police persuaded him to come to the station to give a statement. But he said he would fight the policemen. They

---

*Hills traditionally were considered homes of divinities. The divinities, whether thought to reside in the hills or considered to be the spirits of the hills, were worshipped because of their links to an eternal presence, their majesty, and their inestimable protection as hideouts during wars (Ojo 1966). This practice was retained by the Aladura religion which was an important component of the spiritual, judicial, and reproductive lives of the members of this compound.

tricked him into going to the station by saying that they would not lock him up. Once they got him to the station, though, they put him behind bars. We wives refused to withdraw the charge. When our husband returned home and heard about the incident, he told us that he was sorry. He said that he had not told the guard to kill us; rather, just to discipline us. We told him that he was treating us like goats by putting an ordinary guard in charge of us. Before we agreed to withdraw the case, the guard had to promise to quit.

The federal government wanted to send me and two of the co-wives to Berlin. They helped us obtain passports. It did not work out, because when our husband saw our documents he seized them. I was asked to go again, but our husband refused to give me my passport on the grounds that the other wives would be upset that they were not traveling anywhere. I told him that it was not true as we co-wives were all friends, and the other co-wives had agreed that I should have my passport. When the junior wife wanted to travel, he would not give the passport to her either. Three of us decided to do something about it.

Our husband kept a room to himself; women were forbidden to enter. He kept important documents and our passports in this room. We asked him for our passports over and over. One day, while he was Ibadan, we decided to break into this room. We sent one of the male children in to get the passports. My own passport was not even there. Then the three wives who were involved went to stay in Ọffatẹdo, three kilometers from the house. When our husband returned from Ibadan he asked who had broken his door. Our children told him that their mothers had broken in, stolen his property, and then run away. He went into the room and saw that nothing was missing except the passports.

He took the children to the police station to report that their mothers had stolen their father's things and had run away to Ọffatẹdo. He and the police came to Offatedo. When we saw them we ran inside, but they demanded that we come back out. Our husband told the police to arrest us. We asked why. The police had no reason to arrest us, but our husband insisted, so the police arrested us for breaking into his house. I was carrying my three-year-old daughter, Oluwaṣeyi, on my back at the time. Our husband said that we had stolen his money, but we said that we had taken just our passports. Then I told the police that my own passport was not even there. Our husband slapped me. My brother, Joseph, came to my defense. He told the police that our passports were our own property. Our husband wanted the police to arrest my brother, too, but the police would not because our husband had not reported Joseph as stealing.

We were taken to the police station to make a statement and we were locked up overnight. One police woman asked our husband why he was acting that way to the women he had married. He replied that he wanted to teach us a lesson. She told our husband that nobody knew his wives and that he was doing this only to get publicity for himself. She also told him that there was no law saying we could not have our own passports since we were over twenty years of age. Only a parent can keep a child's passport, she said. "If you have taken it you must give it back," she told him.

Our husband began to worry about what he had done, then, so he went to the divisional police office (DPO) to withdraw the charges. The official at DPO refused to let him, saying that the case was going to court. Our husband offered the official 250 naira, but the official wanted 500 naira. Our husband paid the official and said that he had made a mistake, and we were let go. Our husband was warned not to bring up unnecessary charges.

Once we got home, after being locked up, we wives decided that because our husband could do all these terrible things to us we would have to create our own lives. We decided to never tell him that we were going overseas. Any time we were invited to an exhibition, we simply asked him if we could go to Lagos on business. If he said we could not go, some wives would say okay and stay home, but I would say okay and go anyway. He did not like it when we were not home. Ordinarily, when I returned from a trip he had forbidden me to take, he would be upset. I would just kneel down and beg him to forgive me.

Our husband reported in a local newspaper that we had left him after he had a terrible car accident. In fact, he caused the accident himself. He came home at four o'clock one morning after being with another woman. He said that he suspected that his junior wife was sleeping with his cousin. The junior wife denied it. He threw her down the stairs and said he was going to kill her. As he was looking for a cutlass, she was saying, "My back is broken." The fifth wife and I rushed to her. We all hid, but we could hear him saying, "Where is she? Where is she?" Whenever he fought with one of us, he fought with all of us. He started swearing and said that if the junior wife was not telling the truth he should die in a car accident. We wives went to sleep in the bush. Late that morning he went to Ibadan. He was driving very recklessly, overtaking many vehicles. While the junior wife was packing, preparing to leave, someone came to tell us that our husband was killed in an accident. We left what we were doing and ran to the hospital. It turned out that he was unconscious. I was supposed to travel the next day, but I decided to stay with him. I sent David, another artist, in my place to represent me at the exhibition.

After the accident, I had to take our husband everywhere in my car because he had wrecked his own. I was the one who took him from one hospital to another. Once we took him to the University College Hospital in Ibadan because he said it was an emergency. After he had been given medicine there, he began to tell the attending nurse that he wanted to see her breasts. He told the remaining staff that he didn't want them to treat him because they belonged to the wrong political party. He belonged to the National Party of Nigeria, the political party for Shagari, and so did the hospital staff's boss, so he wanted the boss to treat him.[3] The hospital staff told him he did not need emergency care and sent him away. We then had to take him to another hospital.

He fractured his hip in the accident. Every night the doctor tied his feet to the bed to try to set the bone back into the right position. The junior wife and her friend slept on the floor in the hospital. At night our husband would ask the friend to untie his leg, and they would have sex. The junior wife would wake up sometimes, but she would just keep quiet. One day she decided to challenge him. She told him, "You are going to bed with my friend." "No," he said. "I made a mistake; I thought it was you." While the junior wife was struggling to make his food and to empty his bedpan, he was making her friend pregnant. He left the hospital to return to Oṣogbo because he was afraid that all of his wives would be taken if he did not return.

When he came home I left for the United States. While I was there, all of my artwork burned in a fire at the Raku Gallery. I was stranded. I asked an American friend who was traveling to Nigeria to contact my husband and co-wives and to ask them to withdraw 500 naira from my account or loan me the money to buy a ticket back home. At that time a ticket from the United States to Nigeria cost only 750 naira. The senior wife provided the money and gave it to our husband to buy the ticket. He spent it, and I was still stuck in the United States. Finally, the Nigerian embassy gave me a ticket to return home. When I arrived back home, I was the one who took our husband everywhere. Before I left for the United States, I even took my son, Labayo, out of school to care for our husband. He married two more wives in that period of a year and a half. Before his car accident he demanded that we buy him clothes and loan him thousands of dollars. We wives who were making money had to give him our earnings. And he continued making these demands after the accident. I told him that I was not going to borrow that kind of money for him and that he could take his prick and shove it. He said we were too old for him. He didn't love any of us; he only loved our money. That is how we left him—in good condition. He was making women pregnant.

Nikẹ Davies's home, Ido–Ọṣun Junction, Ọffatẹdo, Ọṣun State, 1993.

**Davies's batik titled "Ọṣun Worshippers."** *(Photograph by Gerris Farris)*

**Davies's batik titled "Women Pounding Yam."**
*(Photograph by Gerris Farris, 1990)*

Davies modeling her signature caftan with her self-appointed description: "Nikẹ, The Woman with the Artistic Brush."

Front view of Davies's signature caftan.

The artists routinely work at Davies's home. Kasali Adeyẹmọ is applying beeswax to white cloth, 1993. The result will be a ladies' caftan.

Davies and Kim Vaz going over the narrative at a Fulani village in Oṣogbo while Iyamide looks on, 1993.

**Davies with the late Sally Mugabe at Akina Mama Wa Afrika's conference "Speaking for Ourselves," London, 1986.**
*(Photograph by Ian Watts)*

To Nike
with much appreciation !
Joan Mondale

**Joan Mondale standing next to her Nikẹ Davies batik. The inscription on the actual photograph reads "To Nikẹ—with much appreciation! Joan Mondale."**

**Davies with longtime friend Victoria Scott.**

**The Nikẹ Center for Arts and Culture, Oṣogbo, Oṣun State, 1993.**

**Emanuel Bamidele Arowogun carving at the Nikẹ Center for Arts and Culture, 1993.**

**An artist specializing in appliqué techniques at the Nikẹ Center for Arts and Culture, 1993.**

Muniratu Bello at Davies's home, Ido–Ọṣun Junction, 1993.

Muniratu Bello holding a batiked shirt she produced at the Nikẹ Center for Arts and Culture, 1993.

# 5

# Iya (Mama) Labayọ*

My great-grandmother always said that her enemies never allowed her to have many children. She told me that I would have as many as I wanted, and she prayed that I would have many. She believed that until I tasted the afterbirth and said I did not want any more children I would have as many as I pleased. According to my great-grandmother, the baby is good luck and the afterbirth is bad luck.

One day during my first pregnancy my abdomen kept giving me a lot of pain and did not stop. I was trying to hide, but my mother-in-law found me and asked me what was the matter. She knew I was about to have a baby, so she took me to the mission house where we had our babies at almost no cost. Most of the wives went to the Christ Apostolic Church's mission to have their babies.[1] Prior to giving birth we would pay something like a nickel a week to the mission, which they would use to buy Dettol [an antiseptic] and other sanitary aids.

On the day I had the baby, there was no money in the house because my husband borrowed it from me to go to Lagos. I had the baby at noon and went home at four o'clock that afternoon. There was no money for a taxi, so my husband's mother and I walked home, a distance of about three kilometers. My mother-in-law carried the baby on her

---

*A woman is usually referred to as "Iya" meaning "mother" combined with the name of her oldest child.

49

back. When people saw me trekking, they said, "Ah! is this not the woman who just had the baby." They said, "She likes to trek." It was not my choice, though. There was no soap or food at home. My mother-in-law went to the trash heap because that is where the vegetables grew quickly. She bathed the baby for the first two days. Later, the other wives helped me for a few days, but they had their own children to care for. I washed my sanitary napkins myself and fetched water. Sometimes the water would spill on me and the baby. Usually, when a woman had a baby her mother would come help her. Since I had no mother, I had to do everything myself. My days were spent looking for food for myself. Since there was no money for milk, I breast-fed the baby. I made *ogi** and gave that to Labayǫ when my milk was not enough. Sometimes I put the baby on my back and worked carrying concrete just to get money for food for myself.

On the eighth day after a child was born, we had a naming ceremony. Our husband gave the child's mother 50 naira, which she used to buy rice and a goat for the celebration. But 50 naira was not enough to cover all the expenses, given the number of people we invited. During each mother's pregnancy, therefore, she put aside money for the infant's naming ceremony. Refreshments must be provided for those who come to greet the mother and her new baby. In order not to be ashamed, the mother usually bought a second goat and additional foodstuffs.[2]

For my first baby, Labayǫ, our husband bought me a wrapper and *buba* [blouse]. The preacher from the Christ Apostolic Church came at about six o'clock, clapping his hands while praying and singing for the baby. He made a speech and gave me guidelines about keeping the baby clean and dressed properly. He told me to make sure the baby became a Christian and to take him to church. The pastor held the baby and asked which name would be given to him. Usually, by this time, the family had already written the name down. We showed the name we had chosen to the preacher. The preacher said the name and everyone repeated it. We named my son Dele Labayǫ, which means "I make my happiness at home." He was named that because his father was not home when he was born; when his father did come home he would meet the happiness, his son, there.[3]

The naming ceremony celebration is a good day for a mother. She

*A pap made from corn.

receives presents and cash from relatives, friends, co-wives, and church members. The money is put inside a bowl and given to the mother.[4] No one is allowed to see how much the mother receives. I planned to use any money I received to buy food. People gave 10 kobo, 50 kobo, and so on. It added up to about 10 naira. I counted the money as people put it into the bowl. It could cause jealousy if a co-wife found out that another wife got more money than she had for any of her children. I remembered that one wife received only 5 pounds, but she cherished it. I knew that I was getting more. Then, to my surprise, when I opened the bowl, it was empty. The preacher from the church had taken all the money.

I went inside to cry. Muni asked me why was I upset. I told her that the preacher had taken the money. Customarily, the church gets about 10 percent of the total amount of the mother's cash gifts, and the mother keeps the rest. I could not tell the preacher that what he had done was not right. I wondered who was going to give me another 12 naira. I prayed to God: "God, this is my first baby and I have been making plans to use the money. You see I have nothing. If you are the only one in heaven, give me more money and presents."

During the evening, our husband invited a musician, Sammy Popular, to play, and some of the artists bought beer. We killed a goat and fed everyone in the neighborhood. The sixth wife put 6 pounds on my head; that was a lot of money in those days. I danced around with our husband. More people came and gave me more money. I had 8 pounds, which was almost sixteen naira, and that was more than the preacher had taken. I was so happy. Then my husband said that he would keep the money for me. He told me that the money was for the baby and should be put in the bank. I told him I wanted to use the money to buy food. He said he would give me more money. I went inside and cried again.

Usually, Yoruba women go back to work forty days after they have had a baby. I went back on the third day to get enough money to buy *ogi* since I could not afford to buy milk. I also had to buy the baby some clothes. I began to carry concrete on my head when Labayo was about three months old, but I did not tell my husband. My husband wondered why I did not ask him for money like the other wives. I knew he would not give it to me anyway. I did not want him to scold me just because of money.

Labayo was two months old when the man who made traditional facial marks and performed circumcisions came to the house. They performed the scarification early in the morning so the baby would not bleed as much as he might bleed in the afternoon. They asked me if I wanted to hold the baby. I said that I could not hold the baby while he was being cut—I would nearly kill the man. The man brought out his board as if he were a butcher, and he ordered us to bring the baby. He said he needed two people to hold the naked child down. They held Labayọ down as if he were a piece of meat on a cutting board. The man cut one section four or five times, then, because it was not deep enough, he continued making up to sixteen to twenty incisions just to make one mark. He stuffed something that looked like charcoal into the cuts.* To "ease the pain" he cut a lizard shape onto the baby's belly. He used a small razor and made little cuts all over. He finished the lizard in about thirty minutes. I just sat and cried. "How can they be cutting my baby?" I said. "I am the one who suffered to deliver him." Then he said it was time for me to "take the pain." I said I was not taking the pain for anybody. They just wanted to cut me. But Muni took some pain because she thought it was true that if you do not endure these cuts—not the facial marks, but the other cuts—you will not have any money to buy food on the way to heaven. Our husband wanted facial marks on the firstborn of each wife. The reason was that he wanted each child to be able to trace his father's family and know his sisters and brothers from each mother.

I went abroad and left my second baby, Vicky, with my husband's mother. By the time I came back, Vicky was sick with the measles. Our junior wife had just given birth, and I usually went to care for her at the mission. We all had our babies at the mission house because it was free, but no one cleaned up after the woman except her relatives. Since my own baby was sick, I only went to see the junior wife briefly the day she delivered. The next day I was told that I had a message and had to go the mission. When I arrived I was told that none of the other wives had been there to look after the junior wife. The cloth and plastic used in the delivery the day before were still dirty, so I washed them. I left my own baby at home, and when I returned my whole body smelled. I sat down just to drink some *gari*. The fifth wife came in the room and said, "Labayọ's mother, come, your baby is dead." I could

---

*The purpose of this repeated gashing of the skin and opening of the wound to which soot and kerosene were rubbed as often as necessary is to deepen the marks and darken them (Negri 1976).

not believe it. Vicky was on the bed. What pained me was that I was just gone two hours to help the other wife and when I returned my own baby was dead. It was just like magic to me. I poured the *gari* on my head. I was crazy and did not know what to do. We took the baby to the Volkswagen car dealer because there was no transportation at our house. Someone I knew from there took us to the mission. I thought that since the baby was still warm she was not really dead. The preacher at the mission prayed over the baby and then said the baby was gone. I just started crying. All the other wives cried too. After Vicky died, we all decided to use medicine in times of illness. Until that time we followed the church rules against using medicine. The church taught that our bodies would become dependent on the medicine, so the only "medicine" you were permitted to use was cold water.

This was in 1975; Vicky was three years old, and my third child was one. Vicky died the third day after I returned home from the United States. My mother-in-law did not believe in using medicine; instead she believed that religion would save the child. After this, I said I did not want any more children, but everyone kept saying I should have more. Our husband did not care if one child died. He said that he had many children and that the dead child belonged to the mother. He never said anything when I went with the junior wife's mother to tell him the baby died (I had to take someone to help me explain what had happened). He did not even say he was sorry. His response still causes me pain today.

They asked me to buy white cloth to bury the baby. They dug a grave near where we had our baths.[5] For three months, I could not go to the toilet close to where we buried my baby. It seemed to me that I should take her up from the ground. A week after Vicky died, our husband wanted to have a naming ceremony for the junior wife's new baby. He wanted to kill a cow, but the junior wife's father refused to participate because it was not proper so soon after Vicky's death.

Each wife had a child that died. Anytime a baby died, our husband accused Muni of killing the baby, but he accused her falsely. He just did not like her, so he tried to make us enemies. He said that Muni was the witch in the house who was killing the babies.[6] Muni was more careful than any of us. If one of her babies was sick, she would make sure that everything was done to cure the baby in time. When the junior wife's baby died, our husband again accused Muni. Muni denied having anything to do with it and said that they could go anywhere to prove it. Our husband took them to a *babalawo* [a priest of the Ifa oracle] who revealed Muni's innocence but told our husband that he had to worship Ogun, the god of iron.[7] When they came home, our husband did not tell anyone that Muni was innocent. He was upset about the junior wife's baby because he was in love with the junior wife. When he loved me, he loved Labayọ, but when he no longer loved me, he did not love my children.

Our children frequently had worms from sleeping on the floor since we did not have beds or bedsheets for them. Our children slept on mats on the dirt floor. The mats were not tightly woven like a rug, so the worms could easily come through. The youngest baby slept on the bed with the mother. The worms could ease themselves through the mat, and the children would cry all night because the worms would be moving under their toes. When we removed the worms the children would be okay.

One night the children were complaining that they were cold. There was no light in the room. We said, "Get up; some of you have urinated on yourselves." The children said they had not. There were about four children from different mothers sleeping together. We put on the lantern and saw a big snake. The snake was moving between the children because he was feeling the warmth from their bodies. There were no men around, so we quickly ran out of the room and got a stick. The fifth wife killed the snake. Her father was a hunter, and there was nothing that she could not do.

# 6

---

# Co-Wife: My Friend
# and My Enemy

We were taught that it was a very shameful thing for a girl not to be a virgin when she went to her husband's house. Our custom required that the mother of the bride hide by the small house where her daughter was having sex with her husband. She would listen to see whether her daughter cried. If she did cry, the mother would know that her daughter was a virgin. Afterward, the mother collected the bride's soiled cloth to show to the other women in the house. If the girl was a virgin, the mother and other women would be very happy. The mother would give her daughter's friends a full packet of biscuits and a full case of soft drinks. If the girl was not a virgin, she would give her friends only half the refreshments. Her friends would be ashamed and say that their friend had disappointed them. The girl herself would not receive all of the money and presents a new wife usually gets. She would be given only half.[1]

But the day before a new bride goes to her husband's house, she has to spend the day crying. I always said that I did not like the crying. If you are crying, it means you are lazy. When you live with your mother, you can get away with everything, but when you go to your husband's house, you are entering a totally new life. You have to work hard. The first two weeks of your marriage, his family does everything for you. After that no one does your washing for you. In your parents' house you can tell your mother that you cannot wash the dishes, and she will get someone else to do it. In your husband's house, you work for many of his relatives. I brought this thinking to my marriage.

Although I had lived in my uncle's polygynous compound, I never expected when I was growing up that I would be in a polygamous marriage. After my mother died, my father never remarried. He also was a devout Catholic. Men who belonged to the Catholic Church in Ogidi did not have more than one wife. The few who did were not allowed to receive Holy Communion.

I did not really agree to marry my first husband. He had a certain way of using "voodoo" if he wanted to marry a woman.[2] It seemed that he could marry her whether she liked it or not. We believed in his power to make things happen to people. He had one room in his house that women could not enter. That is where he kept his "voodoo" medicines.

People use to call my first husband crazy. When he dressed, he would put a can opener strung on a rope around his neck. Anywhere he went he was full of this and other junk. These things made noise when he walked. People always told him to change his style; he would change to something even wilder. They called him crazy, but it was mainly his drinking that caused him to behave this way.

Our husband believed in Ọṣun. He went to the river to bathe and meditate. With his belief and the way he dressed, everyone thought that he was wild. They also thought we, his wives, were wild. Our neighbors abused us when we went to fetch water from the well. They said, "You see those people? They are people who live on a man. They can't do anything. They are living with a man who is crazy, and they too must be crazy. You beautiful girls, why must you live with a crazy man?" We didn't know why. We were always asking ourselves, "Why am I here?" We didn't know either.

I never had sexual intercourse with any man before I met my first husband. He used a trick to get me to sleep with him. He drugged me. One night he put tablets in my drink that caused me to become drowsy, and I fell asleep. He later told me that he had made me this drink in one of the artist's houses that we had just visited.

After that, I found out I was pregnant. Muni had just given birth, although she was not living in the compound with us. That is how I became this man's second wife and she became his third wife. Our husband had a senior wife when I came to Oṣogbo, and I was the next woman to live with them. Muni came to live with us later.

He was always tricking us somehow. For example, he told each of us that he loved that one alone. He said, "I love you. Don't go to your senior wife; she is your enemy." Then he went to the senior wife and said, "Don't tell Nikẹ; you are my senior wife," and so on. He would go to Muni and say, "You are my junior one. Don't tell all these people here; they are too jealous of you." Each of us thought that we were the favorite and should dislike the others. He said that he could not show any of us that he loved us because it would cause fights among the wives.

I thought that he loved me more than he loved the senior wife and I would be happy. The senior wife thought that he loved her more than he loved me and she too would be happy. He said to the senior wife, "This house belongs to you. You see that Muni and Nikẹ—they are going to quarrel. You are the Yoruba one here, your town is Ẹdẹ." So the first wife said that she would always be happy that she owned the house. Then Muni said, "He told me that, since I was the one who had the first boy of the family, my son would become the leader of the house." He told me, "You know you are the one who attends to visitors. I am only trying to be friendly to the others, but I love you more than them. That is why I allow you to know these white people."

One day we co-wives were sitting down talking. I think it was our senior wife who brought it up. She asked if our husband ever told any of us that he loved one more than the other. I said, "Of course he told me that he loves me more than you and that you don't like me because you are the senior. You don't want other wives." The senior wife said, "It's a lie." Then Muni said, "He told me the same thing." That is how we found out his trick and realized that he was using it to tie us down. After that, whenever he said, "I love you," we just threw it in his face that he was lying. It took us many years to figure out his scheme, though.

For a good ten years we wives fought with one another, said bad words to one another, and lied to one another at our husband's instigation. If we did not fight we would never have gotten along. Any woman who says her co-wives get along without fighting is just telling a lie. When a new woman comes into the compound, the other wives might seem happy, but the happiness does not come from the bottom of their hearts. The women may appear to be kind to each other, but behind one another's backs they may be like grass snakes. It took a while for us to become friends. It was only when each wife became busy with her own work and stopped waiting to get money from our husband that our problems began to get solved. We began to see that when we were broke we could sell our work. For example, when our husband got angry with us and wanted to take his table fan from our room, instead of the wives getting mad at one another, we went out and bought our own fan. When we could afford to buy things for ourselves, we stopped worrying about what he said about who he loved best. We wives stopped arguing among ourselves.

Our husband married his first wife in 1965. He was also dating the woman who would become his fourth wife. The first and fourth wives were bitter enemies. Our husband used the senior wife to try and deny that he was the father of the fourth wife's child. Although the fourth wife's child is older than my own, I am her senior. The fourth wife did not bring her child to live with us until 1970. When they went before the court to determine the father of the fourth wife's child, our husband said, "This is my only wife, and I have never gone to bed with this other woman." Then the first wife had to state whether our husband went to bed with the fourth wife. He was just using his first wife to get out of his responsibility.

Another example of our husband trying to pit one wife against another was when our husband said something like, "My senior wife, do you know what Nikẹ said? She is going to do witchcraft against you," but he was just lying to make us fight. The day after hearing this, the senior wife would wake up, and if I greeted her, she would not greet me. She might sing:

> My wife who is my junior wife,
> You can go to your father's house and leave my husband's house for
> me.
> My husband married me before you.

Then I would sing my own song back. Later on the fight would extend to the children. One wife would say to her child, "Don't play with my enemy's child." Then the wives might fight. I had lived with polygamy before, and I didn't care much for singing those songs, but the other women would really argue with each other. Following are examples of the songs they sang.

## I

[In this song, both of the wives are talking about their husband's lover.]

I have known my husband's concubine.
You do not have to show me.
You are somebody who gossips.
I know her already, you woman with a crooked leg.

## II

[This song is sung by the junior wife when the husband likes the senior wife more.]

If you cook fish for our husband, you will not make me do it too.
I will not owe credit because of our husband.
If your soup is sweeter than my own, I will cook something else.
But I will not go bankrupt or rob a bank because of him.

## III

[This song is sung when the senior and junior wives do not get along.]

My senior wife spoiled my name.
She said I sold locust beans.
So what will I use to spoil my senior wife's name.
I am feeling cold, so you, senior wife, use your mouth to cover me.
Your lips are so big, I can use them like a blanket.

## IV

[This song is sung when a wife who does not bleach her skin argues with a wife who does.]

You my enemy who bleaches her skin.
You cannot tell me I cannot come into the room.
I know my husband likes your bleach more.
When I get a cut, you are the one who has poisoned me.
You are the one causing me pain.

## V

[This is a song for when a husband has two wives and a third wife joins them.]

You, my senior two wives, one cooks okra and one cooks vegetables.
If I get stomach trouble, you will be in trouble.
You, two wives, please, I beg you, let me have my own baby. When I
die I do not want my dead body to be thrown outside. My own baby
will be able to take care of me when I die.

## VI

[This song warns against talking negatively about others when one
has not examined oneself.]

You want to abuse me?
You better go and look in your family because your mother is blind and
the person who raised you has leprosy.
So, before you abuse me you better go to your family and look over it
well.

Among ourselves we often fought about seniority.[3] How a woman
meets people in the house determines seniority. A woman can come
from the outside bringing her own ten-year-old child by the male head
of the compound, but she would not be senior to anyone already living
in the house. Seniority is not determined in terms of children's ages.

The fourth wife entered the compound after Muni had had a baby.
She pretended that she had come to help Muni. Eventually, the fourth
wife brought her own child—the one our husband had tried to deny—
to live with us. Muni claimed that she was senior to the fourth wife, but
the fourth wife said that her daughter was senior to Muni's and that she
would agree for me, but not Muni, to be her senior. Once I just got fed
up and said, "Oh, your children are senior to mine; both of you can be
my senior. I don't care."

All of us had boyfriends before we left our husband's compound.
Our husband wanted us to fight with one another so that we would say
our boyfriends' names aloud and in front of him. He wanted to know
our secrets. We abused each other on any topic, but in front of our
husband we never said our boyfriends' names. When we fought, we
never said, "She dates so and so," because if one wife revealed another
wife's boyfriend's name, the second would then promptly reveal the
first's. It was a dangerous thing to cause our husband to suspect that
any of the wives had been unfaithful. One day a wife had some business outside of the compound that required her to sleep overnight
where she was. Our husband accused her of being with another man.

He strung her up like Jesus on the cross and put pepper inside her vagina.

The wife who can make the best soup is known as the one who owns the husband. The husband likes her more than all the other wives. If she can look after the children, keep the house tidy, and not be hot-tempered or fight easily, the husband considers her to be an excellent wife. Some husbands are pleased with the wife who works hard. The husband might say, "My wife washes my clothes, prepares my meals, and loans me money. This one is good," he says. A good wife is willing to volunteer herself and her possessions for her husband's sake. If a wife does not, the husband has a complaint against her. He may say that she works hard and takes care of the baby, but she cannot keep house. That gives him an excuse to go out and marry another wife. The husband then observes the senior wife's behavior to see if she improves now that she has a rival.

I sometimes accompanied our husband when he went to pay bride-price for a new wife. We would go to the parents' house, and they would often say, "We have heard that you are in a polygamous marriage already." Our husband would say, "No, I only have Nikẹ. She will be the senior wife and your daughter will be the junior wife." He married one woman that way. She was from Ṣagamu, which is on the way to Lagos. Whenever we were returning home from Lagos, we would stop in to see her. Our husband also gained wives by paying the school fees of young girls. They could be as young as thirteen years old. In return for sending her to school, our husband would get the girl as a wife.

New women came into the compound, but the ones who stayed were usually pregnant. Shortly after they came in, sometimes before they delivered their baby, they would become a senior wife to a new woman coming in. The incoming wife would always be the one pretending to help the junior wife with her new baby. Our husband would tell the junior wife that he was not going to marry her helper, but it would be a trick. After that the junior wife would find out he had been going to bed with the helper. He would then tell the woman, "This is your junior wife, whether you like it or not."

Sometimes, he would tell me which new woman was his wife. He would not tell any of the other wives. He always said that he told me because I was not jealous. It would be a secret between me and him. He felt that if he told the others they would spread the word around.

Whenever a new wife came, our husband said that she had to come and see me. When a new wife first came into the compound, she would kneel down to greet a wife and call her by her first baby's name. To me, she would say, "Good morning, Mama Labayọ." The new wife would show respect by helping another wife to sweep her room. Or, if a wife was doing something, like grinding pepper, the new wife would offer to finish the task. New wives did not have to do this all the time. They just did it to show respect. For example, if a wife had visitors but was not around, the new wife would make food for the visitors so they did not have to wait for food. A new wife could not be depended on all the time, though. If you did not ever refuse the favors they offered, they would say, "This one wants a slave." A few new wives would say, "To hell with the older ones." Usually, if a woman didn't have a baby for our husband, he would not claim her as a wife.

I prepared food for the new wives. The other wives did not know that I was cooperating with our husband. I went along with him just to please him. I always tried to please him so that he would not get upset with me like he did with the other wives. I would just talk to myself: I told myself that if I was jealous, he would not go to bed with me. I did not need to sleep with him to get what I needed for myself and my children, though. I had my own way of earning money. If I wanted to go to Lagos to sell my work, he would say, "Okay, you can go. On your way home, stop and say hello to the lady in Ṣagamu." He would be happy and would say, "When you get there, tell her so and so."

There were a lot of things that he told me that he did not tell the other wives. When he wanted to marry his seventh wife, he told me a year in advance. Everybody knew he had a girlfriend in Ibadan, but they did not know who she was. He made arrangements for her to come during my daughter's birthday party. Our husband told the other wives that she was a sales agent for one of his products. They did not know that she was already a junior wife. By the time the seventh wife came to live with us, three weeks later, our husband already had another wife in Ogidi living with his mother. He told me that Ọṣun had given him a wife. I asked him how Ọṣun could have given him a wife.

Our husband was driven to have these wives because of what men here believe about women. Once a woman has had three or four children, men say that she is finished. They compare her to a flat tire. Women feel that the tire can be repaired to look like new, but the men say that it will never look like new. Once a woman has a baby, men think that she is not as good as a woman without a baby. Men need a new woman to charge their battery and keep them young. A man will not go with an older woman. He feels that her old blood makes him older. If he goes with a younger woman he thinks he will look younger.

Our husband told me about his relationships because he knew I would not get jealous. I knew that if I became jealous, it would not change him. He always made the jealous wife the loser: if her friend came to visit, he would not let her see the visitor; if he knew there was something she wanted to do, he would spoil it. Once you released yourself and acted like a person who didn't understand anything, he thought you were a dummy. Then he would take you as a ride, but most of the time he would let you do what you wanted to do.

Whenever I had money, I told him that I had nothing. If he wanted to borrow money, I would tell him that I would borrow it for him. He and I both knew that he would never pay it back. I would loan him my own money and let him think I borrowed it to pay back myself. He always said he loved me more than the other wives. Of course he did not. He was just able to take more advantage of me than of the other wives.

We used to hide from one another the fact that each of us had a boyfriend. Only the sixth wife did not. Little by little each of us began looking for a nice man. If one of us was dating the wrong man, the other co-wives would advise her. Once a man was interested in me. I told him that I was married and that my husband was very jealous. He said that he was married too but that he and his wife were separated. Whenever he saw mixed-race children he always loved them. He said that he had been in Africa a long time and wanted to marry an African woman. I said, "If you want to marry an African woman, do not consider me." I was so scared that our husband would find out. I told the senior wife, the fourth wife, and the sixth wife about this man. They were impressed with this man who dated me for six months without touching me. They sometimes went with me to the man's house. Finally, they said, "Nike, why don't you take it." I began to spend all of my time at this man's house. After some time my co-wives said that I had to choose either to go with this man or to stay with our husband. They said it was getting dangerous for them in the compound. They no longer knew what to say to our husband, because I was no longer staying in the house. Every day they had to lie for me, and they could not continue. I saw their reasoning. It came to the point where I had to choose, so I chose to leave completely, even though there were powerful reasons to stay in the relationship—my children, his "voodoo," and my love for my co-wives. I did not have to legally divorce my first husband, because he didn't pay bride-price for me. The only real marriages are those in which the husband pays the bride-price. When it is paid, the couple has to go to court to dissolve the marriage. When a husband doesn't pay, he doesn't have the right to divorce in court.

When I left our husband, I had to leave my children, and I went to live with my second husband. A one man–one wife relationship was strange to me. I was used to waiting my turn to see my husband. A wife in a polygynous marriage had to do a lot of work for him before she got a smile from her husband. For instance, sometimes our husband would be afraid of the bad flies that lived in the toilet area. So, when he didn't want to risk getting bitten, he would have a bowel movement in his room on a piece of paper and call one of the wives to throw it away for him. I worshiped him like a god for sixteen good years. He never thought that I could be free.

He behaved as if it was only him whom God had created. He had his own republic in the house. He was our judge. If he upset us, he would tell us not to speak. With my second husband, things are different. If I go out, he worries about me. If I travel, he calls me. At first it was so new and strange. When my second husband went to work, I was at home alone. The children were at school, and I was at home doing my artwork. I was very lonely. In polygamous marriages, the co-wives shared their concerns, and there was always someone to talk to. When I moved in with my second husband, I had no friends. I used to say that my work was my friend, but sometimes you want to explain some things to a friend. If you talk to yourself, people think you are crazy. I started playing music. It took some time to get used to. Now I love it.

# 7

---

# I Will Not Mention My Enemy's Name

Any money made from the sale of artwork on display at our husband's gallery that was produced by me, the other wives, and our husband's apprentices belonged to our husband. We never made any profit unless he was away from the house when visitors came to make purchases. However, I was making money that our husband did not know about. I used to send my brother, Joseph, to Kaduna to sell my works. He would leave them at the embassies for prospective buyers. I also used to send my brother to Kano and Lagos to sell for me. My friend Victoria Scott used to sell my work and keep the money for me in Lagos.[1] Our husband never knew that I was putting money aside. He was just so happy that I seldom left the house. Occasionally, our husband would find out about the extra money and he would take it away. He then would be convinced that I would not be able to work. He was always surprised that I still managed to produce work.

Victoria Scott befriended me shortly after I came to Oṣogbo. She was teaching art history at the Yaba Institute of Technology in Lagos. I met Victoria at my husband's exhibition at a foreign diplomatic mission in Lagos. She saw me and we started talking. Before then, she had begun to read about my husband and the other Oṣogbo artists. She wanted to become familiar with Nigerian art outside of Yaba and

Lagos. Victoria liked my embroidery more than my batik. She was the first person who bought my embroidery. She also thought that it was very good to see a young woman striving to be a serious artist. There were so few women entering that profession.

Victoria encouraged me from the beginning of my career. She came from Lagos to see me every weekend. She persuaded me to take my work to Lagos. She asked me to sell it. She even took my work to America. She convinced her friend to arrange an exhibition in a gallery in New York in 1971. My first husband happened to be in America at the time and went to that gallery and ripped everything up. Then, in 1972, she arranged another exhibition at the Tribal Gallery in New York for a little group of Oṣogbo artists; my first husband did not know about that one.

I was too shy to speak English, but Victoria told me not to be afraid. She felt that I should use any English words I could, and she would try to understand. Eventually, my husband selected me to greet our guests because my English was improving. As my friendship with Victoria grew, she would tell me about a life different from the one I knew. She used to ask me why I was still in a polygamous marriage. I thought I had no other choice. She tried to convince me that after I had traveled a bit, I would not like polygamy. I could not imagine that. I loved polygamy because we co-wives loved one another. The problems started when our husband came home. He would tell one wife to sleep with him, and then he would tell her in private that the other wives were practicing witchcraft against her.

Victoria asked me how I used my money. Since I was working for him, any money from the batik sales was his. He even borrowed the money I earned when I carried concrete for the construction workers. Whenever he wanted to borrow money, he was friendly to me. He would say, "Hello, dear, my wife." I was so happy then that I was getting attention that I loaned him the money. I didn't know he was just using his silver tongue to get money from me. He could not borrow money from the other wives because they would not do any extra work. They just depended on him. If he did not give them money for food, they ate nothing.

Victoria discouraged me from giving my money to my husband. Yoruba women don't usually give their money to their husbands, but because of the kind of man he was, no one was able to keep any money in that house. He would not sleep if he knew money was in the house.

If we hid it, he found it. If I put money in the bank, he took my checkbook, forged my signature, and withdrew my money without my permission.

My husband began to dislike Victoria. He accused her of ruining his family. He did not want us to continue our friendship. When Victoria and her husband came to our home in the initial stages of our friendship, my husband entertained them. One day, however, my husband just began acting crazy in front of Victoria and her husband. They were offended and left. They asked me and my junior wife to come to the place where they were staying during their visit to Oṣogbo. We went when our husband left the house, but when we returned he was already home. Victoria and her husband dropped us off at the house. When he saw them he shook his ax and told them not to come back. He threatened to use the ax on them if they returned. I had not wanted to tell them about his character before—about how he used to beat us. This time, he started beating the junior wife. He took a fork and stuck it in her eye. Blood immediately began rushing out. He was running about doing wild things. The other expatriates who were with Victoria insisted on taking the junior wife to the hospital to find out if she would be blind. The doctor told her she would not lose her sight.

In 1976, Victoria began to encourage me to divorce my husband. She told me to give her some of my money so she could save it for me. The reason she gave was that whenever I wanted to leave my husband, I would have money of my own and I would not have to worry about what I would use to survive. I would not leave him, though. I was afraid of him and I was afraid that he would make me go crazy.* He used to scare us with all his "voodoo." Since I had no mother and only one brother, if I went crazy, who would look after my brother and my father? My father has no money. He is a farmer.

During this time, one Aladura man from the Christ Apostolic Church said to me, "Go write it down; you are going to suffer here, but after, you will get somebody to help you.[2] The time is coming when they will be talking about you on the radio and in the newspaper. First,

---

*There is widespread belief that some who are mentally ill have been cursed by an enemy who has hired the services of certain herbalists with the knowledge and "medicines" to induce insanity (Prince 1964 and Simpson 1980). For an example of a recipe for a substance thought to produce insanity when injested and its accompanying incantation, see Verger 1971.

you are going to suffer. Do not think this man is going to help you. Somebody will come here, maybe when he is away; that is the person who is going to help you." He revealed this to me around the time I was really tired of the abuse and disorganization in the compound and I was thinking to myself, "This is it. I am finished with him." I contemplated joining the police force. They would pay me a salary. If you are a bit tall they take you. You don't have to be all that educated, and you don't have to pay for the training. They take anybody who has finished primary grade six. When I heard the prophesy, knowing what I had been through, I decided to stay. The same day, the preacher told our husband that he saw him with many wives, but in the future he saw everybody disappearing. The preacher told our husband that he had married us for business. "In the future." he told him, "you will have one wife."³ Then he came back to me and said that I was going to marry a white man. I did not believe him because I had no interest in white men. I was so scared because our husband always said that if we went to bed with another man he would know. Another preacher in Ibadan told me that I was going to have a house. I started laughing. At the time, I did not have 10 kobo to my name. How was I going to build a house? These two predictions gave me comfort, though, and I always reflected on them in times of trouble. The preacher in Ibadan told me to write it down—that I was going to be somebody big but that I should not change my character. He told me to continue working hard; that is how I stayed with our husband.

A female magistrate in Oṣogbo used to tell all us wives, "You are like children to me, but the way you are now, I see this man is only using you." She persuaded us not to spend our money on things that did not last, such as televisions. Rather, she told us to invest our money in things that would not spoil. We did not know what would not spoil. She told us, "Use your money to buy land. I used to be married to a man with two wives. I never told the man that I had land and that I had built my own house. When I left him, I moved into my own house." Then we knew what would not spoil.⁴

She introduced me to the doctor who sold me the land. This same man sold land to several of the other co-wives. The magistrate served as the mediator between the doctor and myself. I gave her the money. She processed the papers and kept them with her. Later, she arranged for me to meet the justice who had helped me get all my documents— my certificate of occupancy, for instance.

The building of my first house was a slow process. My father's brother (from the same father but not the same mother) brought his son to Oṣogbo to go to school. He put the boy there so that I could check on him. I could never check on the boy, though, because my husband would not let me go out. When my uncle visited his son, he also visited me. He would tell my husband that he was taking me out, and we would go to Lagos and other places. He would also give me 20 or 30 naira. One day he said, "Tell me, my sister, is there anything that I can do for you?" I said, "A white woman who is my good friend has saved about 1,600 naira for me. I would like to begin building a house." He said that I did not have enough to build a house. I told him that I had already bought the land. I needed him to ask another brother from Ogidi who worked in Lagos to sell me cement at a wholesale price. He took me down to see the man. The man agreed but made me promise not tell anybody, because people would demand that as he had helped me, he should help them. He gave me an allocation of twenty tons of cement. He told me to sell it and said that any gain that I made I should use to go to the United States or to change my life. This was the way he could help me since he could not give me money. I paid him and took the cement back to Oṣogbo. I directed the trucks to the church so that my husband would not know about it. From the church the cement went directly to the people who would buy it, the retailers. I did this three times for a total of sixty tons of cement. With the profit, I started the house in Oṣogbo; it took ten years to finish.

Our husband did not know anything about it. I told the fifth wife but none of the other wives. I was working harder than ever, producing and selling much of what I made. I had a friend in Kaduna who sold my work for me. In a month, she made more than 3,000 naira. I added this money to the profit I made from selling the cement to raise the foundation for my house in Oṣogbo. I wanted to tell our husband's mother. I loved her very much. I loved her like my own mother. My co-wife discouraged me from doing so. She said, "Don't. A mother is always a mother to her child. If you tell her, she is going to tell her son. Keep it a secret. If you tell her, she will tell her son and he will come and wreck everything."

My husband never knew I had a house until I divorced him and he reported me to Timi, the king of Ẹdẹ. My first husband thought my second husband built the house and said so to the king. The king told me I had to confess. I said, "You can see that the house is not new. My second husband is on salary and cannot afford to build me a house." I told him that I had been building it little by little. I said that I did not want to tell my first husband because the other wives would believe that he had given me the money for the house and become jealous. Tears came from my first husband's eyes. He could not believe it.

While I was still living with my first husband, whenever I wanted to go somewhere, I hired a taxi to take me there. The first time I wanted to go to Lagos, I hired a taxi. Our husband looked out the window and asked the man what he was doing. The man said he had come to take me to Lagos. Our husband replied, "You wait for me." The man thought our husband was coming to greet him, so he prostrated himself and said, "Welcome, sir." Our husband ordered the band boys to remove the man's car tires and beat him. He was accused of being a robber. After that, no taxi driver would take us co-wives anywhere. To get a taxi, I pretended that I was leaving the house to go to the toilet. I did not wear good clothes. When I got near the main road, I changed my clothes. One time our husband saw the vehicle with me in it. He jumped in his car and caught up with the taxi at the petrol station. He ordered the band boys to loosen the man's tires and to beat him. The man told me not to hire him anymore. I decided that was all I could stand.

At an exhibition I held at the Italian embassy, I made enough money to buy a Volkswagen Beetle. By that time I had finished my little house that only the fifth wife knew about. I told the fifth wife that I wanted to buy a car but that I was afraid our husband might burn it. I feared that he would be suspicious of how I had acquired the money. On top of that, he would want to borrow the car. The fifth wife asked, "If you are scared of him, how long will you remain that way? Go and buy the car. Let him get upset. When you buy the car, go and buy him a bottle of schnapps and give him some money." He came to me soon after and asked me if I had some money. I had 4,000 naira. I asked him how much he wanted. He said 500. I gave him the money, and he went to Lagos.

With the remaining money I went to the car dealership, which happened to be in front of our house. I told the manager at the car dealership that I wanted to put the car in my brother's name. The manager said, "If you use his name, tomorrow he will be claiming the car. Although you are of the same mother and the same father, he is a young boy. When he sees a car he will not be inclined to continue working hard. You have suffered for your money before bringing it here. I am going to put your name and your husband's name on it so he won't be upset. If you use your husband's name, he will be proud." For a complete two weeks, I could not bring myself to go and pick up the car, because I was too afraid. The fifth wife finally convinced me to go ahead. That is how I bought my first car, in 1979.

When I went to get the car, I could not drive. The fifth wife suggested that I take one of the band boys to drive for me. When we drove the car to the house, our husband wanted to know where I had gotten it from. I told him that I had just bought it. Before going to the house, I asked the older people in our area to help me beg him so that he would not get upset. I asked an older man, a neighbor, who had a lot of money, to talk with him. He told our husband that it was his own good luck that his wife bought a car. He could always use it—anytime he wanted. My husband was still upset. He asked me why I would buy a car when we had many things to use money for? I said that the taxis charged too much and if I bought a car I could always tell people that he was the one who bought the car and that he allowed me to drive it. He said, "Loan me some more money." I knelt down and said, "Forgive me if I have offended you."

I showed him the receipt, which had both our names on it. He told me that I should have told him about it before I bought the car. I told him that I was afraid that he would have said "No." I brought out whisky and 250 naira. (I had waited until he was broke and really needed money and there was nothing that he could do.) So, he kept the 250 naira. He kicked the car and left.

For three good days he spent the money I gave him. He drove the car and I bought the petrol. I had to get a license plate, and I asked him to help me. In the meantime, he was telling everybody, "This is the car I just bought for my wife." In some places he told people it was his own car. He used my car because his own was wrecked. My car was like a toy to him because he never suffered for the money; I did all the work. Later, he bought a used Beetle. Once, while he was driving recklessly, three tires blew out. Instead of using my car, he removed the tires from his car, jacked mine up, and put my tires on his car. I complained, but people said I should not say anything. The fifth wife grew tired of this. She said to him, "You go out, and when you see us along the road you do not pick us up. Now you've taken her tires." She said she was not going to stand for that anymore. He said to her, "I know that Nikẹ is the one who is your husband. I don't want you in this house." He hit her anytime she spoke the truth. Once he soaked the whole vehicle with petrol. The fifth wife said, "Mama Labayọ, Mama Labayọ, this crazy man has wet your car. Bring your key. He is looking for matches. He has been saying that since you have the car you don't stay in the house anymore; you just go to parties." I moved my car before he could get to it and went and parked it at my house. For five days he asked to borrow the car. I told him that it was at the mechanic's. He said he went to each mechanic in the town. He never found my car. Though he said I went to parties, that is not what I did with my car. If I wanted to go to Lagos to sell my work and others wanted to go or had their work ready, I took them and/or their work.

Our husband chased away all the drivers I tried to hire. He would not allow me to learn to drive. If I said that I wanted one person or another to teach me, he said no. He just wanted me to leave my car in the yard. Finally, I hired a young man who had been in the theater with us. He had no license. I always said to myself that we would be lucky if the police did not arrest us. Eventually the driver did receive his license.

Whenever I wanted to go Lagos or the fifth wife wanted to go out, we would take my car. Once we all went to Ogidi for Christmas. Our husband told me not to tell anybody it was my car and to say it was his own. I agreed. The other wives were angry. They told me that it was not his and that I should not let him have it. They called him a liar and a robber. Whenever people said to him, "Well done" (that he had plenty of money to buy a car), he said, "Thank you." When he said this to my father, one of the wives said, "Don't mind him. It is your daughter's car." My father was so excited. He wanted to go for a ride. I sent the driver with him. Our husband was very upset. The other wives said that I should just let him get upset. "He can't be claiming something that is not his," they told me.

In the early 1970s I began to go to other countries. This influenced me to change my behavior and helped me to see my life differently. For example, I always used to wear my batiked dresses. When I began to get interested in other men, even while I was married, I started wearing western clothes. In Nigeria, the more you wear western clothes, the more men think you are a bit "westernized." When you wear a wrapper and *buba*, they say you haven't been out of the country. I am one of the few women who wore trousers in Oṣogbo. Women did not wear trousers in the more traditional areas. Wearing trousers implied to the local people that you were a prostitute. When I first started wearing them, I was always called a prostitute. I would be ashamed then, and I would go home and take them off. Later on, I stopped caring. I continued to wear trousers because they were comfortable. After I met the man who became my second husband, I stopped wearing westernized clothes. Now I wear only clothes that I design.

But not all things in the West are better than they are here in Nigeria. When I travel, the people I encounter are often very nice. But as an African I cannot help noticing the prejudice. I always wear either clothes that I have designed or other African dresses. I have nothing to hide. Our clothing is so beautiful. I might be getting on the subway, though, for instance, and someone will say, "Oogabooga."

When I give lectures about the art of Oṣogbo or my work, some listeners ask questions about our bodies and way of life. "Do you have tails? Do you live in trees back home? Do wild animals attack people?" One person even asked me what we did with our deceased. I replied that we eat them. Everyone laughed. "What do you with your dead people?" I asked. A person who is dead is buried, I said. I explained that when people die in our village we spend more money than do Westerners on funeral celebrations. People drink and have a good time. Everyone is made aware that the deceased has many children. When I first said that we eat our deceased, the audience members were so happy because that is what they wanted to hear.

Being a successful and single woman in Nigeria is not easy. Nigerian men want to marry you because you are making money. But they like to control women. They want the woman to be under them. I know because I travel and see that women have more freedom in other countries. I see how men behave in other places. In this area, it is men's rights that are foremost.

People in Oṣogbo still have trouble believing that I am successful enough to have built this second house at the Ido–Oṣun junction. Many people say that my white husband has built me a mighty house. Once one of his old girlfriends asked him why he allowed me to stay in the house alone. She wanted to have a room in my house. It is *my* house. *I* built it and *I* own it. This is what I try to teach my girls—to have their own houses so that no one can come in or put them out. Once I was having my car washed. The boys washing the car saw a vehicle that belonged to the company that my husband works for. They said, "Ah! Look at that white man. You know he took that artist's wife and built her a house." They did not know me. I said, "I know this woman you are talking about. She is my good friend. The woman works. She does not depend on a man." They said, "Ha! Her first husband bought her a car. She was the one he loved most, and she still left him." They refused to believe that a woman could be hard working. They said, "That is how women are. They take what a man gives, and they leave." Then, they said that the woman married a white man. I said, "How many single men in Nigeria would marry a woman with three children already? If she tried to marry him, his family would refuse her." The family would believe that the woman would use up too much of the man's resources.

But men's rights in this country have begun to affect my second marriage. Now my second husband is trying to control me. He says that because he has lived so long in Africa, he wants to behave like an African man. He wants to get another wife. I always say no. People say I should let him, though, because he is protecting me. It is hard for him to accept me as I am. He encourages me to jerri curl* my hair, because he does not like to touch it when it is natural. I do not know how long this marriage will last. I cannot really predict. I do not know what is going to happen tomorrow. I feel I that I need a figurehead to protect me so that I can do my work and so men won't be saying, "I want to marry you."

Men's rights in Nigeria are so powerful that even the women who introduced all these men to art are never mentioned by them. There is a woman artist in Oṣogbo who has become like a mother to me. She is Suzanne Wenger, an Austrian woman who was using wax and doing batik long before I came to Oṣogbo. My first husband promised to introduce her to me when I first came to Oṣogbo. He said that this woman would be willing to help me become an artist. For years after getting to Oṣogbo, I never saw her or her work. She, along with Georgina and Ulli Beier, started the art program in Oṣogbo and taught the other male artists, such as Ṣangodare Ajala, our husband, and some others.

I did not meet Suzanne until one day when visitors came to the

---

*This is a curly hairstyle produced through chemical means and is popular among Blacks in Africa and the African diaspora.

gallery and our husband was not at home. The visitors wanted to see Suzanne. I took them to her house. She told me that she did not know who I was. I told her that I was one of the wives of one of the artists she helped train, and then she greeted me.

I was not really close to her until after my husband had a serious car accident in 1984. One day I saw her, and she said that she wanted to come and greet him to see how he was doing. I picked her up from her house and drove her to ours. She said she wanted to see my work. I was able to get close to her only after I left my first husband and married my second one. Suzanne treats most of the artists as if they are her children. She is like a mother to me. I always feel like I have a mother. If anything happens to me she can fight on my behalf, and if anything happens to her I can fight on her behalf. Once a woman wrote an article about me that she sent to Suzanne. It was a bad article. Suzanne confronted the woman, who in my presence had said that I was nice but in the article said that I was bad. When I saw Suzanne's reply to the woman, I felt all my sorrow leave, and I did not have to respond. Our husband did not want his wives to go to Suzanne's house. So many of these Oşogbo artists pretend to be the master of their art. Each man claims to be the greatest artist and the originator of the art. We always told these men, "Suzanne is your boss because she is an artist. Georgina is an artist and Ulli is a writer. They are the ones who started the art." The men responded, "Suzanne and Georgina are women; they cannot be our leaders."

Once an exhibition was arranged for all the Oşogbo artists. The men complained that only five of the exhibitors were really Oşogbo artists. The curator wanted to include Suzanne, who she knew had trained many of the men. The men claimed that Suzanne was not an artist. I told the men that it was only through this woman's and Georgina's efforts that they learned about art. It was Georgina who told me she was the teacher of these men, but the men never acknowledged her. They never gave her credit. I give her credit, because if it were not for her I might not have come to Oşogbo. Before Suzanne and Georgina came, there were no Oşogbo artists, and they used their own money to feed the men. They bought them materials and maintained their workspace.

# 8

---

# Strong Women

There were just a few women who were a bit successful in Ogidi. There was a woman named Mary who sold beer. People who made any money would go there and drink. From that money Mary bought her own house. Some of the men talked her into letting them live there. She married one man and had two children. When he began to mistreat her, she married another man. All the people called her a harlot. She became well-off later, and those same people went to her to try and borrow money. She just told them to go to hell.

Two or three women owned their own farms. My mother's sister was one. She grew plenty of yams, but most of her money came from palm oil. She hired twelve women to work for her during the palm oil season—from around June through August. She even hired men to work for her.

There was a bitter fight in Ogidi over the starting of a new market.[1] My mother's sister, who was senior to all the daughters of my mother's father, was opposed to the new market because it would take business away from the old one. The old market was right in front of her father's house.* Some of the traders wanted to start a new market a few miles away. The new market would destroy the old market. When

---

*In traditional times, markets were located across from the king's palace (Ogundipẹ 1978).

they fought for the old market, she said, "This is my own house, my father was the king of the town, and this is where I will remain. This is the market my mother grew up with. This is the market my father grew up with, and even though my father is dead I want to keep this market."

On market day, those supporting the new market did not attend.[2] Those supporting the new market had influence with the police, so market day turned into a big argument. The police took my aunt and her supporters to jail in Kabba. She bailed herself out with her own money. She paid 10 naira to bail herself out. I was there the day she was arrested. I went home from school that day to be with her. If my mother had been alive, I thought she might fight for her father's position. My aunt greeted me and then said, "Go to your school; this doesn't concern you." She was a strong woman.

People believed that the struggle over the markets caused her death. They thought the opposition killed her with "voodoo." During the struggle she said she did not care if she died. She felt it was more important to fight for her rights. When she died, people said that she lost her life for nothing. As a woman she should not have been fighting for her father's rights, they said. She started the foundation of her house before she died. She said that when she died, she wanted to be buried in the house she was building, not in her father's. That is where they buried her.

Ogidi was split in two over the old and new markets. My father supported the new market. He said a new market would bring money and recognition to Ogidi. He thought the word would spread to the surrounding areas that on market days the new market had everything. The people who supported the old market stopped speaking to the ones who wanted the new market. Those who did not own homes were put out of the ones they rented. My father was run out of three different houses in three months. Those supporting the new market were called rebels. The father of one of my classmates had many houses in the town. He allowed us to live in one—a mud house—since no one was staying there and looking after it. My father and brother became the caretakers. Supporters of the old market asked my classmate to run us out. He refused because my father and brother were taking good care of the house. My father lived there until I left for Kabba in 1967. I told my father that if I ever had money in my life, I would build him a two-story house. He would have an "upstair" house where he could stay up and look down at his enemies. He asked me what I meant. I told him that this was a proverb: The people who chased him from house to house have flat houses. His house would be taller. He wished me good luck.

Women like my aunt are considered brave. Such women have a leadership role in their town or church. They are strong. They stand on their own two feet and tell others what to do. Nobody scares them. If someone tries to tell them to do something that they do not want to do, they tell the person to shove his or her money in their asses. They say they are not doing this or that, and they do not do it. They are strong enough to face a woman or a man. They do not care if they lose their lives or their husbands. They just do what they want to do. They are very powerful.

Before some women become strong they have to struggle in battle. Queen Amina was strong, and she fought in war.[3] To be thought of as brave, a woman has to have her job in her own hands. She has to have a good standard of living by herself. She has to have a good husband, not a crook or a duper. If she marries a duper, he will spoil her life. If he dupes someone, the victim will come and say bad things to him, and the wife has no right to talk back.

When I was growing up there were not many women who were considered brave in Ogidi. Only if a woman was put in charge in church or in the town would she tell all the other women what to do. I learned more about strong women when I came to Oṣogbo. I did not see these women, but I heard stories about them. I once heard about a woman who could drive a car—any type of vehicle at any time of the day or night. There was a story about strong women in the next town, Ẹdẹ. Normally, women blended cassava by hand. When the engine was introduced in Ẹdẹ that automatically ground the cassava to *gari*, it inflated the price of *gari*. The people with the engine raised the price from three pence to six pence. Many women got together and said that they would not buy the *gari* from the people who used the machines. After the women reached an agreement, the wife of the king continued to have her cassava blended by the people with the machines. The townswomen said, "You want to show us that you have money. We are reporting you to the king." The king told his wife that she had no right to go against the wishes of the majority of the women.

Some strong women are good, but some are really wicked, and people think they are witches. In our legends, there is the story of an *iyalode** of Ibadan named Ẹfunsetan Aniwura.[4] She was a wealthy woman who had no children. She forbade all of her slaves, male and female, from having children. The penalty was death, not for the men but for the women. One male slave and one female slave were intimate with each other, however. The female slave, Adetutu, continuously reminded her lover of the consequences of pregnancy, but he told her that she could not get pregnant the first time they had intercourse. He assured her that she would be okay. Whenever the *iyalode* sent the female slave to the farm, her lover would meet her and they would make love. Soon, another female slave noticed that Adetutu was pregnant. She became very alarmed. She and Adetutu went to inform Adetutu's boyfriend. He decided to kill the *iyalode*. The women became alarmed because they believed that the *iyalode* was all-knowing and could see the future. The man's intention was to have the cook poison the *iyalode*'s food. If that failed, he was going to use a cutlass to chop her head off. He was very sure of himself. The man prepared the poison and persuaded the *iyalode*'s cook, who was Adetutu's friend and confidant, to place the poison in the *iyalode*'s food. The *iyalode* told the cook that she had seen the bottom of the chicken (i.e., that her secret was out). The *iyalode* knew that her food had been poisoned. The *iyalode* forced the cook to reveal the man's name and to eat the poisoned food. The man was ready with his cutlass, but the *iyalode*'s guards killed both the man and his girlfriend. The community was very angry over the way the *iyalode* was killing her slaves. They sent two powerful men to her, but she used her magic to enslave them. Then the townspeople prepared their own sorcery to force the *iyalode* to obey them. More townspeople went to her and said, "Today is the day for you to come out." She replied that they were only men, but she was water and there was nothing they could do without water. The people said they were vessels that could survive in the water. Many words passed between them. Since the townspeople banded together, their magic was stronger than hers. They were able to capture her. Immediately they took her to the king and freed her slaves. She preferred to die rather than becoming a slave, though. So she used a potion that she had left in her skirt to poison herself. That is how the townspeople got rid of her. She was a wicked strong woman.

---

*\*Iyalode* is an elected woman leader who represents women's economic and political interests in local governments.

Some strong women fight for themselves, and others fight for women's progress. One of my co-wives in my first marriage was a strong woman, but she did not use her power to stop our husband from beating us. She used it only for herself.

I am not strong enough to be considered brave. I would love to be one. I would be proud of myself. I would be able to live on my own, independently. I would not worry that people were coming to attack me. I would stand on my own or fight for women like myself. I would fight for women's rights.

Strong women remain in the memories of people. Their names will never perish whether they stand for good or evil.

### Postscript, 1993

In 1990 I did not feel that I could be a strong woman. But now that is changing. The more I stand on my own and have independence in my work, the stronger I become. When I was with my first husband, I could not say that I was strong. I had to ask for permission for everything. Even my second husband tried to control me. He cannot do that anymore. I don't know how to put it. Now, I can do more of what I like. To get strong, you have to work hard at it; if not, you are just going to be kept down.

# 9

## The Woman with the Artistic Brush

In the 1960s people thought that artists were crazy or dropouts from society.[1] Back then, most people would not allow their children to become artists. They thought all artists were drug addicts. We, the artists, dressed differently from the local people since we designed our own clothes. That caused the local people to insult us, saying that we could not change our clothes to fit the new fashions. They called us all idol worshipers because we did not attend Christian or Muslim services. We believed in traditional religion—the religion we had before these other religions were introduced. In the past, people who sold firewood were the poorest people in the society. If the local people saw an artist (who worked in pen and ink on wood) carrying plywood, they assumed that he or she was poor. Only now, as people see that I am using a car, are they bringing their own children to my art center. Now that they see that I have built a house, they believe that the job of artist is a job that pays, and they let their children come to my center. Members of the center are generally unmarried women and men under the age of thirty.

When I left my first husband in 1986, I worked alone in my own house. There was a man who used to buy plastic from me. He said he had a daughter who wanted to work for me. She wanted to clean my house. I told him my plan was to have a studio where girls who had nothing to do but who had an interest in art could be trained. I say that I "train" the people who come to my center because you cannot teach art; you can only encourage it. Besides, I wanted people to talk to and I wanted people around who had had experiences similar to mine. I told this man these things, and he said that he would like his daughter, Bumi, to learn from me. I took the girl in, and I laid her hand in art. My son was already a practicing artist, and he was happy to train Bumi whenever I had to travel. After some time, a second young woman came, and then others joined also. In the beginning, I gave my students the cloth and other materials for their artwork. I wanted them to be able to sell their work, so I took it with me to Lagos. If I did not go to Lagos, my students would not make any money; most of the people I sold to knew me through the gallery in my first husband's compound. That is why I opened a gallery myself; it was just because of the students. Even when I was not around, visitors could come to the gallery and buy the students' work. Now the students can stay in Oṣogbo and make their own money. When students began coming to the center from around the world, I wanted to keep my home separate from where the students learned about art. So my little house in Oṣogbo became a studio as well as a gallery, and we officially opened it in 1988.

At first we used the name the Oṣogbo Artist Cooperative, but Ulli Beier suggested to me that using the word "cooperative" would imply that we were associated with the government.[2] Since we are a nonprofit organization and we do not offer a certificate, we named the center after me. There is no set length of time for students to study, and they are free to come and go anytime. They must fill out a form indicating how many years they wish to study, so their parents cannot accuse me of stealing their children. This is their agreement. Some people train artists for a set length of time, offering students "freedom" at the end of the apprenticeship period. Most charge for instruction. I do not want my students' money. If my students are better off in the future and work as artists for a living, they will always remember me and my children.

I do not charge my students a kobo. I ask that they bring their own materials. If they do not have enough money to buy materials, the center tries to buy materials for them. Currently we are not taking new students; we have about forty* and we do not want to overcrowd

*This section is based on interviews conducted in 1990.

ourselves. The senior students teach the junior ones. We also have professional artists in certain areas, such as batik and carving. They also teach. Even if foreign students come and I am not at the center, they never feel my absence because there are so many people around to help them.

The students live by rules when they join the center. If they steal and we find out about it, they are dismissed. If a man beats a woman, he is dismissed. If women have fights with each other, they are suspended. We usually have group meetings every month. If someone is offended or something is going on that someone doesn't like, that someone voices his or her feelings at the meetings. We resolve the issues at the meetings, and there is no fighting.

Most women in Oṣogbo do not think art is for them. My center is there to encourage women to try their hands at art. When people commission us to do work, or when they buy the work of an individual artist, the artist keeps his or her own money. I do not take it. I built the studio and gallery and pay for the electricity and maintenance of the property. Still, all of this is not enough to attract these women, or to inspire the ones who are already members of the center. Recently, a foreign artist, Georgina Beier, came to the studio to teach the members how to use *adirẹ* cloth to make quilts. Georgina grew weary with the women. The men learned faster and were more enthusiastic. The women complained that the work was too hard and that they had never sewn before. I told them that the men had never sewn either, but they were trying. It is not hard to take a horse to the river, but you cannot make her drink. I always tell the women that if a man buys a car, the women should tell themselves that they too can work hard to get one. If a man can build a house, the women should become determined to build one too. Then the man and the woman will be equal. But if the woman says that she is afraid that people will talk about her if she tries to achieve, then the power will be given to men.[3]

I used to be afraid of what people would say if I became too independent of my husband. But then I began to travel and to see the world. In the West, the husband and wife both work. The baby goes to day-care. Each spouse has a salary. Each contributes to the mortgage. The income comes from both sides, so the husband cannot send the wife out of the house. Here, pooling resources does not work. If I have my own car and my husband says I cannot go out, after he goes out I can take my own car and go where I want. But if I were a housewife and we had one car, it would belong to my husband. If he said that I could not go out, I would have to stay home. A woman must work hard and have her own things. Even if men's rights are foremost, a woman can have her own property. She needs to have her own things so she can feel strong by herself.

It is hard to change the women's ways of thinking. The women in the surrounding villages live on 3 naira a day. For example, there is one woman who used to sell kola nuts to make money. I asked her to come to the studio to learn how to change the color of old lace. I told her that she could make more money than she earned now selling kola nuts. She felt that her husband would not agree and would send her out of her home. I told her that she would make her own money and that it would not matter. She could use the extra money to pay her own rent and take better care of her children. She, like so many others, has not participated in the center's activities. Even when the women see my success they don't really believe that anyone can make money through art. They feel they have to carry their trays, making just a few naira every day.

Some people say that batiks are crafts. When you make an original batik and do not make copies, it is not a craft. It is art. The stories my batiks tell are those I heard in childhood and convey a moral message. The story about green snakes hiding in green grass tells of how wicked some people are. Other stories tell about how a poor person can become rich in her later life or about behaviors people have that destroy their lives. The story about a rich junior wife and a poor senior wife, both of whom have children, touches me, because when I lived with my great-grandmother we were so poor that we sold banana leaves that we cut in the bush to buy locust beans. We hardly had 1 kobo—which is the equivalent of 1 American cent. In the story, the senior wife was so poor that she went into the bush to fetch leaves and firewood. She laid her baby under a tree while she worked. When she came back she saw that a bird had carried the baby into the tree. "Where's my baby? The bird is going to kill my baby, and I am suffering just to get something for the baby to eat," she cried. She sang to the bird, "Please give me my baby. I know you are the leader of all the birds. The baby is on the ground because I am poor and I am looking for firewood. I did not put her on the ground because I do not like her. I love her." She began to praise the bird and then asked to be forgiven if she had offended him. The bird said, "I know of your problems." He gave the baby back, along with diamonds and jewelry, and the woman became rich. The junior wife saw her. She who could afford to buy so many things for her baby thought, "I am going to the bush to find the bird." She told the bird, "Come and take this baby; I don't want it anymore." The bird came, took the baby into the tree, and then threw it back to the junior wife. The baby died.* The junior wife was jealous of the senior wife. She had never complained when the senior wife was struggling and the junior wife had more, though. Their lives were not equal. I could give each of my five children the same thing: 100,000 naira, the same kind of car, the same amount of cloth, the same type of house; some will manage well and some will mismanage. Others won't care because they never suffered for their gains. People who work hard will become rich. You can give anybody money, but their character may force them to lose it. Once you have suffered, you will be able to manage your money well. My great-grandmother told me this story.

The snake charmer story always appears in my work: In a village in the east, every year they would tie down a beautiful girl who had reached the marrying age. When it came the turn of the king's daughter, the king called the whole town together. He told the townspeople, "We have to find out if the snake is doing good. If it is not helping us, I do not want to sacrifice my daughter. Why are you offering human sacrifices for an ordinary snake?" He said that the snake had become something evil, something they worshiped. Anybody who could kill the snake and defeat the devil snake would be given half of the king's property and his daughter in marriage. No one from that village wanted to try. There was a wanderer who walked from town to town whose mother had given him a special knife that was to be used when he was in danger. He passed through that town and saw the beautiful girl tied down. The people explained what had happened. The wanderer said that he would kill the snake. The townsmen taunted him and then left him alone. The snake wrapped itself around the wanderer and tried to bite him. He remembered the knife his mother had given him. He took it out of his pocket and killed the snake. Before dying, the snake called to another snake. The man ended up killing all the snakes, and the villagers stopped using their daughters for sacrifices.

I have a good memory for stories. That is what motivated me to draw. I have my own ideas about what the snake looked like, how the

---

*An account of this story can be found in Ellis (1894/1964).

man remembered his knife, and how the snake tried to make the man fall down so that he could swallow him.

Many of my drawings are based on the "dream of the palm wine." People have to climb the palm tree to get the wine. The wine is popular because it is local and even poor people can afford it. Some even make it at their own farms. People believe that it is a good cure for fever because it makes the sick person urinate. In most of my drawings I include how the palm wine is brought from the farm.

I usually center much of my art around the mothers of twins. Until recently, in some parts of Nigeria when twins were born they were killed. Twins were considered bad luck.[4] Women asked, "Why are you killing these twins? They do not bring bad luck." The children would be killed at night and in secret. Now people feel that it is good luck to have twins because people will pity your condition and will give you money. I focus on the old stories, too, and draw events from daily life, such as village scenes, how people make food, people coming from the farm, and so on.

I am an artist. Women who make ceramic mugs and traditional pots and sell them to the local market are craftswomen.[5] They know that they will make some small amount of money every day. A mug costs only about 5 naira. But I may sell one piece today and not sell anything else for the next three months. I may have many visitors, but they might buy nothing. Everyone has some small change to buy a craftswoman's ware, but those women will never make big money. They only make enough to cover their expenses. I do not think they make enough of a profit to buy personal things for themselves. They may owe creditors. I do not buy on credit. Even if I do not make a profit, I seldom owe anyone anything. Most people who buy crafts do not even know the craftswoman's name. Craftswomen do not put their own names or even the name of the town where they work on their crafts. I put both my name and town on my work, so when visitors come to Oṣogbo and ask for me, they are directed to my house or gallery.

When I sell things, even if I don't make a profit, I never lose. All my life there has never been anyone to whom I could turn. The only thing I could do to support myself was to sell goods. I always made sure that if I had 5 kobo, I could make it 10. It may take a while, but it will happen. I learned from my great-grandmother. She was a weaver. When she was commissioned to make a cloth, she would tell her customer how much it cost and require a deposit. She would not risk losing anything because she took the deposit.

I want women to come to the studio to have an experience. They only refuse to change because their eyes are not open. They have not traveled to see how other people live. If they traveled and saw how other women live, they would no longer stay under control. They would be willing to do something for themselves. Married women believe that once they have children they cannot learn anything else. Besides, their housework takes up all their time. But that is how you suffer, suffer, suffer, for the rest of your life. You have to work for your children, you have to work for your husband, and you have no time to work for your own self-improvement. Some women here are thirty years old but they look like they're fifty, just because of the housework.

Then there is the problem of the husbands. Once women are married their husbands will not let them come to the studio. The men know that as soon as the woman knows how to work and get income of her own, they can't control her. When she has nothing, she has to kneel down before her husband. The man can say, "You are my wife. I don't want that woman to teach you." He knows his wife would be okay on her own. I cannot actively recruit women because the husbands would accuse me of stealing their wives. Yet if the women want to come, they are welcome.

# Appendix

## Muniratu Temilade Bello*

Muniratu Temilade (precious crown) Bello was born in Ogidi, Kwara State, Nigeria, in 1953. She married her first husband in 1969 at the age of 16. She had four children with him: Gbenga 22, Toyin 21, Funke 19, and Bumi 18.† After spending nine years with her first husband, Bello left him in 1978. She remarried into a polygynous household and had four children with her second husband. In 1988, when I first interviewed Bello, she said her husband treated his wives well. Her new husband set her up as a seamstress. The interview was conducted at her shop in Oṣogbo. Kikẹ Ọdẹyẹmi served as interpreter, and Michael Oduntan translated and transcribed the interview. When I interviewed her a second time, in 1990, Bello had left her second husband's compound because the enmity among the co-wives was too much for her to bear. Her sewing business had been unsuccessful, and she was working at Davies's studio producing batiks. Her son Gbenga and Kings Amao, a member of the Nikẹ Center for Arts and Culture, served as interpreters during the 1990 interviews. Gbenga transcribed and translated the interviews, which we conducted daily in a small room at Davies's studio. In 1993 I reviewed the previous interviews with Bello for further clarification. Michael Oludare served

---

*The English translation is "Two bright stars of God."
†These ages are from 1990.

89

as language and cultural interpreter. At the time of our last interview in 1993, Bello was employed under the auspices of the government-sponsored Better Life for Rural Women project, had a son working in Germany, had resumed making batiks, and was enjoying living away from her second polygynously married husband and co-wives.

* * *

Before I was born, my mother went to a *babalawo* from Ilorin who lived in the our village. Mother was in her tenth month with a stomach so large and legs so swollen that she thought she was carrying twins. The *babalawo* informed her that she was carrying one girl and foretold that I would want to marry someone of my choice and that my parents should not stop me. This caused a big argument between my mother and father. When I grew up and wanted to marry the person I selected, my father refused to consent, but my mother reminded him of the *babalawo*'s prediction when I was in the womb. The *babalawo* had also foretold that after I was born my mother would become prosperous. Around the time she was carrying me, my mother opened a store from which she sold foodstuffs. She no longer has the shop, because some witches caused a heavy wind to roll full-force into it.[1] This destroyed the merchandise. After that, things did not go well for her. People in her day were jealous of other people's progress and looked for their downfall. My mother went back to the farm and started selling skulls and bones of animals, birds, and snakes.

As I grew up, I noticed a mark on my body that neither my brothers nor my sisters had. My mother said that when I was a baby I fainted anytime they gave me *ẹkọ*.[2] At first they did not realize that it was the *ẹkọ* that made me faint. Instead they thought that I was an *emere*, a baby with an evil spirit.[3] They cut my body and put pepper in the incisions to stop me from fainting.* Later on they stopped giving me *ẹkọ* and then realized that the *ẹkọ* had been the cause of my fainting.

I know that I am a child given to my parents by the river deity. My parents consulted the priests at a river when they went to beg and pray for children.† As an infant, I did not like to be bathed in

---

*A combination of incantations and incisions (gbẹrẹ) are used to drive away troublesome spirits (Makinde, 1988).

†The Yorubas believed that immortal spirits inhabited perennial streams. These streams were worshipped. Stream water was given to infants to drink in an effort to impart the spirits' immortal qualities to babies, who had the highest death rate in the community (Ojo 1966).

warm water. Some babies are like that, preferring the cold water instead. When they bathed me in warm water, I would feel cold and my skin would become very rough. This meant that I was a child of the water.

As a little girl, I loved going to the farm with my dad. Since he was the only male child of his father, he inherited a large farm with many palm and orange trees. He grew cocoa, coffee, yams, cashew and kola nuts, and vegetables, such as tomatoes and peppers. We had fowl and ducks that we let roam about to find their own food. My brothers would help him, but during the harvest period he hired people to help.

I used to help my mother on the farm with the weeding and the palm oil production. We produced large quantities of palm oil and other products that I helped my mother to sell. My mother supervised the women who assisted her in palm oil production. After the palm nuts were cut from the tree, the women covered them with palm fronds. Eventually, the nuts would get soft. The women hit them with sticks until the nuts were free from the shells. When the women finished cooking the nuts, they poured the resulting substance into a rock with a large depression in the middle. (As our society became modern we beat the nuts in a mortar using a pestle. The cooked nuts were poured into a gourd with a cement bottom.) Once the nuts cooled, two to three of us would wash our legs, step into the hollow, and begin to press the nuts with our feet. Water was then poured into the hollow, and the women pressed the entire mixture with their feet. Next, they used their hands to mix everything together, and this released the oil from the nuts. They used a plate to remove the foam that came from the nuts. The liquid was cooked again, thereby changing it to palm oil.

My major role was to fetch water from a stream about a half kilometer away. This was the water that was poured into the hollow with the cooked nuts. Processing palm oil requires a lot of water, and it required two to six people to go to the stream ten to twenty times, even for small jobs. In my own case, I would go about five times and then my mother would tell me to rest. My *akengbe* [calabash] was not very large, but it was appropriate for my size and age. It was about one foot in diameter and one foot in height with a round mouth. We plucked these from the tree. When my calabash was filled with water, I could not lift it. Others would help me to put it on my head. Sometimes as we walked to the stream we sang festival songs. For example, we sometimes sang, "You are welcome, my husband, you are welcome," referring to masqueraders. The adults talked about the possibilities of getting work on other farms. I played with grasshoppers and other insects, and the adults would rush me along, saying that they would not help with my *akengbe* if I lagged behind. I sang another song: "My flower, my flower, if you want to buy my flower it is ten shillings." The others would shout at me to hurry up because time was passing. They would say, "What kind of fucking flower are you holding?" Then they would take the flower and throw it on the ground.

When we harvested cocoa, my job was to remove the beans from the pod. My father and brothers would cut the cocoa with a cutlass. Usually we produced eight to ten bags of cocoa. The beans were placed in a basket (that was about three feet in diameter and one and a half feet in height) over a calabash. The liquid that dripped into the calabash was sweet. I liked it very much. I had to remove the beans from the pod myself and allow the liquid from the beans to drain into a calabash because no one would let me drink her "cocoa water." I shelled just enough to obtain cocoa water to fill about two beer bottles. Then I went back to play. Cocoa water is alcoholic. After drinking it, I would become intoxicated and go to sleep. My mother thought that I was sleeping because I was lazy, but it was really the drink.

Sometimes the cocoa and palm nut harvests overlapped. Three to six women would work with the palm oil production and six to eight women would work with the cocoa because it was so plentiful. As payment, my father gave each woman a tin of palm oil. The remaining oil was stored in big pots about three feet in diameter and two feet in height. We had eight pots like this. We kept one potful of oil for cooking and put the rest up for sale. Although my mother sold the oil, she gave my father the money. But she would determine the rate. If she sold it for 30 naira, my father would receive 25 naira, and my mother used the other 5 naira for my school fees.

We had coffee on our farm too, but I disliked participating in the harvest work because small insects, such as ants, would sting and bite us. My father started using Gammalin 20 before we plucked the beans from the trees.[4] We took the beans to a flat surface and left them for about two weeks to dry. We never employed more than two people to help us because more could easily steal the harvest. We pounded the beans using a mortar and pestle. We placed the beans on a tray and then blew away the shells so that we could sell just the beans. We all accompanied my father to the place where he sold the coffee. We went about eight miles on foot, carrying the coffee. My father had a bicycle that he put his load on, but the rest of us—me, my mother, and my siblings—walked with our loads, resting periodically. I used a small Semovita bag, which is about two feet high and six inches in diameter, to carry my coffee. We went to a house with a measuring machine, and my father received about 40 pounds for a large sack of coffee. We usually had four bags of coffee, but sometimes the animals from the bush ate some, and we would have only three bags.

We picked the oranges on the farm ourselves and sold them from home at the rate of six for one kobo. We handled the peppers the same way, keeping some for our own use. My father did most of the work harvesting the kola nuts. After cutting the pod of the kola nut we would remove the inner cover and place it in a basket. Mainly my father, but sometimes my mother, would sell it. The Hausa people were the ones who bought from us.

I worked at the farm in the afternoons and on weekends when I was attending school. In the evening we went home to our house in the village. The house was built with mud and had a bamboo ceiling. The first building consisted of four rooms and a kitchen. My father had a room in a separate building. Our compound was fenced in, and in our yard were orange trees and herbs. My father used the herbs to treat childhood and other illnesses that befell our family or neighbors.

Father had three wives. The junior wife died when I was very young, and his senior wife was very old. She did not work on the farm, but she could take anything she wanted from the farm. My mother was his second and favorite wife. My father had been a traditional worshiper before he converted to Islam. The senior wife would not convert to Islam, which made my father angry. My mother did convert. Mother also had been a traditional worshiper. Every April her family took palm oil to the rock called Qrunro.[5] The one who was possessed of the spirit of Qrunro would lick the oil off the ground with her tongue. Failure to propitiate the spirit of the rock resulted in the family having sore throats. Even after converting, mother still ingested palm oil in April. She would either pour palm oil on her wrist and lick it off or pour it in a calabash and drink it. Whenever her throat became sore she would say that it was from not taking palm oil. She would appease it by taking some oil.[6]

Before mother converted to Islam, she often consulted *babalawos*.

Once, my brother, her second born, could not walk, and the assumption was that he had a disease. My mother and brother were left in the care of a *babalawo* in another town on the other side of a bridge. Mother ate the little food that she had brought with her until it was gone. My father took foodstuffs to them, but the *babalawo* kept the food for his own use. The *babalawo* ordered my mother to work on his farm. At the farm, there was nothing for either her or the child to eat. Once she cooked some cassava and a little later she started vomiting. She had to be carried back home. When my father came to visit her, my mother complained of the way she had been starved. She refused to remain in the *babalawo*'s care any longer. Father went to explain to the *babalawo* that he was taking his wife home. The *babalawo* instructed my father to have my mother select seven stones when they got to the riverbank. She was to place the stones in the water for the baby to drink. As they approached the river, father reminded her of the *babalawo*'s instructions. She refused to follow them, saying that it was not the river that caused her to have a baby. Mother left my brother's cure to fate and her belief in God. After a month passed, the baby started walking.

Mother taught me how to turn wool into thread, which we used to weave cloth. She taught me other things, such as how to take care of a house, care for babies, set up a business, and perform circumcision on male infants. I cannot perform the circumcision because I do not like using a blade, but I can clean the wound. I have not forgotten how to do these things, but I just do not practice them.

My mother did not like people who gossiped or did bad things. In fact, she used to tell me one story of two wives who were accused of doing immoral things. Neither one admitted to being guilty. The husband took his wives to town, to a rock that contained water. Two spirits lived in this rock, *Odiḍẹrẹ* and *Aluko rere*.* The spirits knew which of the wives was lying and would kill the guilty one. The wives climbed seven steps to get to the water inside the rock. On the third step they sang, "We are coming to you to tell us who has done the bad thing." The *babalawo* performed a ritual that made the spirits become alert. The junior wife was asked if she had done the bad deed. She denied it, and the *babalawo* took her into the water. The first time the junior wife came out of the water, one side of her face was painted red with *osun*. The second time she came up, the other side of her face was

---

*The spirits took the form of a parrot and a woodcock.

painted white with *ofun*.[7] The third time she came up, spirits had put beads on her neck, hands, and legs and had given her many gifts. Her family was very glad when she emerged from the water. The *babalawo* urged the senior wife to tell the truth before it was too late. She denied doing anything wrong. The first time she came out of the water, the hair on half her head was shaved off. The same thing happened the second time. The third time her blood colored the water. My mother told me this story so that I would not do bad things.[8]

My father loved me very much when I was a little girl. He took me to the mosque with him and sometimes asked me to eat with him. I loved my father's war stories. He told one about the war that took place when he was very young between our people in Ogidi and the Nupe (or Tapa) people.* The Ogidi people hid in a cave that was situated at the side of a mountain. Inside this cave was a mortar and pestle made of stone that still stands there. Anytime the Ogidi were attacked they ran and hid in the cave. The Nupe usually won the wars against the Ogidi because they fought on horseback. The Nupe took the defeated Ogidi people captive.

Then the Ogidi people worked out a system of action for when they were attacked at night. Without making any noise, they touched the body of anyone who was sleeping. If the person woke up, he or she would go and hide. Those who did not wake up were captured by the Nupe. There came a time when my father's grandfathers felt that the war was taking too great a toll on the Ogidi people. They went to an Ifa priest to consult the oracle. They learned that in the cave dwelled a female spirit who could help them. They were told to weave a large white cloth that they used to cover the top of the mountain. The Nupe people would not be able to capture them. The elders complained that the strategy had been used before without success. The Ifa priest did not listen to their complaints and ordered them to do as he said. The cloth was woven and the Nupe people were prevented from climbing the mountain. They fell on their backs and lost the war. The Ogidi captives were returned, and the Nupe were taken captive.

The other story that my father told was of a great hunter named

---

*The hostility between the Nupe and the Kabba-Yorubas reached its zenith in the nineteenth century. The Nupe repeatedly raided the Kabba-Yoruba in part to obtain people to enslave for the trans-Saharan trade and for indigenous use (Belasco 1980).

Abejide in our town. Once the men went into the bush to kill an elephant, but they did not know how to do it in such a way that they would not be attacked. Abejide decided to wait until the elephant passed excrement from his anus. Abejide entered the elephant's anus and moved on to the abdominal cavity. He destroyed the elephant's internal organs, causing the animal to die. He returned to tell the people of his feat.

My father did not like people who gossiped or stole. I had a friend who stole something, but when my father found out, she was not allowed to visit our compound or to continue our friendship. My father did not like his sister, Ajikẹ, a woman who had six children, five of whom had died. Everyone believed that she had killed her children, and they considered her to be a witch.[9] Even when she visited our compound, my father dodged her or pretended that he did not know she was around. I also believed that she was a witch. Why else would five of her children die? She did not act like she cared very much. It would probably have killed her if she had thought about it. Some of her children died of fever, and another died from a wound that was inflicted at the farm.

Father respected elders, strangers, and people with a lot of knowledge, irrespective of their age or stature. He especially liked his mother's junior sister, Ọmọye. She resembled his mother and was nice and generous. She advised my father on many important issues.

I was very happy as a child. I was free to do anything I pleased. I was the last born, and my mother took proper care of me. I never wanted my parents to quarrel. They would exchange words, but my father never beat my mother. I wanted them to get along well, because if she became too angry with him she might leave and he would never permit her to take me. I would surely suffer. My mother bought me a small wooden doll. I played with this doll, putting it on my back like a woman carrying her child. I attached a bicycle wheel to a chair and pretended it was a sewing machine. All the little girls my age came with their cloth, which I pretended to sew. They gave me small stones as make-believe money. We also played hide and seek. I had both boys and girls for friends. My two best friends then and now are Yekutu and Asumọu. We spent a lot of time together. We used to climb the mountain in back of our house together. We cultivated our own small farms and went there when we had time. Or we just played in my father's large courtyard. We played a game in which both girls and boys participated.

We removed the outer shell of the coconut. The coconut was put on the ground about five to eight meters from where everyone was standing. Each contestant was blindfolded and given a cutlass. The first contestant would approach the coconut where she or he had last sighted it. The crowd would shout for the person to move to the left or right. Whoever cut the coconut in half was the winner.

As I grew older, my father required that we all go to the farm and work. I no longer received special attention. I preferred to work with my mother because I could rest anytime I wanted to and play or climb trees. My father would never agree to that. I was my mother's favorite child, partly because I was the last born and partly because I resembled her. My mother used the money from her own purse to send me to school, since my father refused to take that responsibility.[10] In those days, popular belief held that educating a female child was a waste since she would just go to her husband's house. My father did educate my senior brothers. One brother went to Qur'anic and European schools and is now a primary school teacher in Kwara State. Another brother dropped out of the Qur'anic school because he did not understand Arabic. He went to a European school, then on to the Nigerian Defense Academy, and he is now in the army in Kaduna State. The last brother went to both types of schools and graduated with a bachelor of arts in history. He teaches secondary school in Kwara State.

My senior sisters were sad and a bit jealous when they found out that my mother was sending me to school. They used to ask me to write letters for them. Sometimes I would be busy playing or working and would refuse. Then they would get angry with me. I would feel guilty and stop what I was doing in order to write their letters, but they would just shout at me.

I started primary grade one in 1964. By then I was already grown up. Mother could only pay my fees up to standard grade four, so I was not able to attain more education. To earn money, my mother worked on someone else's farm; they would pay her and give her food. If my father had contributed, today I would be able to achieve many things. Back then I dreamed of being a nurse or a teacher.[11] I stopped caring for my father when he made it difficult for me to continue my education. I can remember during one harvest, I was sent away from school because I owed 1 naira 25 kobo. My father told me to go to the farm, but I refused. That day, my mother had already bought some cassava that she intended to process and then sell. The money she earned she would use to pay my school fees. My father beat me that evening because I refused to help him. My father used to tell me to not think only about books. He felt I should know about farming, and he taught me how to plant maize, vegetables, and okra. He taught me by demonstrating the techniques. I was not taught how to plant yams because women are not allowed to plant yams.*

I went to live with my brother to continue school. There I attended Qur'anic- and European-style schools. It was then that I experienced my first period. I knew nothing about menstruation. When I saw that blood had stained my pants, I ran to tell my sister-in-law Rabiatu. She started joking with me, saying that I had slept with a man and that she was going to tell my brother Aminu. I was so afraid that there was nothing that I could do to convince my brother of my innocence. I just packed and ran back home. About three days later my brother and his wife came to bring me back to their home. My sister-in-law tried to assure me that she was joking, but I just refused to believe her. Everyone was laughing, but no one explained anything. This made me more upset, and I thought I was going to die.

I was now sixteen. Because of my period, my father made up his mind that I would marry a Muslim man who wanted to pay bride-price. I objected to this. I did not want to be Muslim. I knew that some men kept their wives secluded. If a Muslim wife was going somewhere, she had to cover her face. This is the main reason I did not want to be Muslim. I also did not want to marry the man because he was old and had several wives.

My other sisters did not oppose the choices my father made for them, and they had very elaborate weddings as a result. In the case of my second sister, Rukaitu, I served as her attendant. I was ten years old at the time. The elders from the husband's family came and begged for the release of the bride. Our family asked how much the bride-price was and whether it had been paid. His family replied in the affirmative and indicated that they had paid 60 naira. This was the rate in 1963. The next day the bride would be decorated with *osun*, a traditional red paint. A woman who decorated brides in our area made *ilaali* (henna with water). The *ilaali* was applied to the bride's nails and the backs of

---

*Traditionally yams were regarded as men's crops and only they were given the prerogative to cultivate them. Women's crops included cassava, coco yams, and pumpkins (Okonjo 1991).

her legs. About seven young women escorted the bride to her husband's compound and carried her belongings. We stayed at his compound for about three days. Our task was to prevent the husband from seeing his new bride. Our parents came later to pray for the bride and to bless the new wife and husband. My sister was dressed in traditional cloth woven from the women's loom. Her face was veiled in a fine white cloth. I held her hand and wore very good cloth. Before she entered her husband's house, I was to collect a small basin to wash the bride's feet. I did not go until I was given 1 naira to do it. After I washed her feet, we entered the house.[12] The people rejoiced upon her entrance. She was invited to sit down, but I refused to let her go. I was given another naira, at which point I let her sit down. She was asked to remove her white cloth, but I did not allow it. The husband gave me 1 naira and 50 kobo, and I let her remove her veil.[13] The women in his family wanted to remove the clothes she was wearing, but I would not allow it until they paid me 2 naira. Then the women changed my sister's clothes. I stayed with her for about ten months. By that time she had delivered a child.

That was how I was supposed to marry too, but I could not. After my father decided to give me to this old man, I ran away every day. Before father woke up in the morning, I would leave the compound, returning after he went to sleep in the evening. Mother, who did not support the idea of giving me in marriage to an older man, gently opened the door for me to come in and sleep.

I was feeling desperate and, soon after, I married a man I selected in order to avoid the Muslim man. I met my first husband when he came to Ogidi. He came with Waidi, a student of his and boyfriend to my friend Yeputu. Yeputu said, "We should go and visit our brother," referring to the man I would eventually marry. We used to call him brother because he came from Ogidi. I had no idea he would be at the place Yeputu was taking us. When we arrived, the man said to me, "Ah, my sister, how are you? For three days now I have not seen you; it's been quite an age." He greeted me something like that and asked me about my brother. My brother and this man were friends prior to our meeting. He asked if I would come back and see him in the evening. Although I agreed, I did not go. The man sent Waidi to call me, and I went then. My father was furious when I visited this man. He quarreled with me and beat me.

The man came to visit me every weekend. We would play and have a good time. He really loved me. After visiting this man often, I made up my mind to marry him. Since my father would not agree to my marrying him, I went to Oṣogbo without his permission. I felt bad that I was not married in the traditional sense, but I wanted to marry this younger man as fast as I could to be rid of the older man. My husband-to-be wanted me to come too, and he gave me 1 pound (about 2 naira). We considered 1 pound a lot of money. I used it for my traveling fare, obtaining 2 shillings (about 20 kobo) in change. That was after deducting money for the taxi and other things; I still had 2 shillings left!

When I arrived in Oṣogbo, I used to watch the artists, since I did not know how to do pen and ink drawings. Later on I started coloring in other people's sketches. My husband-to-be had two wives at the time: Mama Labayọ and his senior wife. We used to play and joke together. We were very friendly. The third day after I arrived I had my second menstrual cycle. I became pregnant the next month and gave birth to my first son, Gbenga, on January 23, 1970. The woman who became the fourth wife arrived after I had Gbenga. She came under the pretense of offering to help me with child care. But soon she brought her own daughter. There was a lot of animosity between this woman and myself. Once, when we were all working on the veranda, the junior sister of our senior wife saw the fourth wife enter my room. The junior sister watched the woman put soda ash into Gbenga's food. We all rushed to the room because we heard the two women struggling.

Once our husband brought back caps from a trip for Labayọ and Gbenga, both of whom were just a few months old. He did not bring anything back for the fourth wife's daughter or for the rest of the children. The fourth wife was very angry. Her daughter was older than my son by two years, but the fourth wife had come to live in the compound after me. The other co-wives and I never accepted her as our senior wife because she had not been living in the compound before any of us. We fought about it constantly until she agreed to be ranked as our junior wife.

When I first came to the compound, our husband had little money, but he was nice. He used to do good things. Later on he started picking fights with me all the time. He started making trouble with me when he began to pay the school fees for the woman who became the sixth wife. Although he planned to marry her, he married his fifth wife before marrying this young girl. Our husband met his sixth wife when she was thirteen years old.

Our husband usually fought me when I asked him for something. Whenever I said, "Please give me," or if I wanted to buy something for a particular child, he would say he had no money. He would turn it into a quarrel, and then he would seriously beat me. There was one occasion when I asked him for money for baby food; this caused a quarrel. Things were very cheap at that time. He said he had no money. He picked up the pot of soup we had just prepared and poured it into my private parts. Then he beat me very seriously. He tore all my clothes off; I was completely naked. Today, were it not for the rights and the privileges of the children that I had for him, if I saw my first husband on the street I would not greet him.

Even though we, his wives, were working for him, he did not pay us. Whenever he was paid for a job, he alone would spend the money. We almost turned to stealing in order to eat. We went for a long time buying foodstuffs on credit when he would not give us money. We went about picking palm kernel fruit here and there. We were always looking for dead fowl around the refuse depot during the time of the disease that killed the fowl. It was very rampant at that time. We ate the fowl because there was no food—nothing at all.

Once he wanted to have an exhibition of some of his works. We were then doing a great deal of work for him. At the time there was no light in our house because the Nigerian Energy and Power Authority had turned the power off. I took the work to our next-door neighbor's house because they had light in their house. When I finished the work, I gave it to him. As usual, there was no food in the house and no money to buy any. He and his sixth wife were eating soup with chicken in it in the sitting room. I came in to tell him that I had finished the work. He thought that I had come just to look at what they were eating, so he did not answer me or say anything. I repeated myself, saying, "You are the one I am talking to." He did not answer me. I left the work on the ground and went outside the house. I climbed the tree that was outside the house. I just sat there and stared because neither myself nor my children had eaten. We were all hungry. A few of the wives went to buy bread on credit. As they were walking along eating it, they offered some to me. They told me that they had just bought the bread on credit and that I should do the same. I said jokingly, "Is that why you are following one another, walking and eating bread like prisoners?" I was merely joking. Our husband bolted out of the house and said I was making jest of him and his wife. He used a sport shoe to beat me on the back. He beat me so seriously that I could not stand up straight again for a complete two weeks. I had to bend over to walk. How many experiences can I even recount? How many can one recount? This man beat me with such brutality with that shoe that my back, my very back, was bleeding. The scar is still there. It continues to cause me pain. I continued to live in the compound because I thought if I was courageous I could endure until he changed.[14] But nothing improved; everything just got worse. I did not want to leave my children. I knew they would suffer in his compound if their mother was not there to care for them. But it occurred to me that staying in that house would lead to my death. Life would be terrible for my children if that happened. So I moved out, but I did not move too far away, so that I could continue to see my children.

I left this man in 1979 after ten years of living with him. One day I packed my belongings and rented my own house. I took my husband to court. The divorce took three months because my husband did not want me to go. He bribed court officials to delay the case. I also paid, so that the process could get moving. I have always been a determined person. Once, as a child, I decided that I would go to another town and visit my uncle. I informed my mother, who tried to do everything she could to stop me. She seized my clothes and reported me to my father, but I still went. I decided to leave my first husband because I could no longer cope with the problems he posed. I married another man with more than one wife and chose, due to the other wives' behavior, to rent my own house, though I still remained that man's wife. My second husband refused at first. He did everything he could to stop me. I am now living on my own, though I am still his wife.

I believe that I can be successful in life. I have my health and the knowledge that other people have left poverty behind. There was a woman in my hometown who was very poor. Her name was Mary. She sold beer, and everyone considered her a harlot until she became wealthy. Eventually, she made it and surprised everyone. When she became affluent, people stopped saying bad things about her. I am hard working like she was. When I married my second husband, he asked me what I wanted to do. I had an interest in tailoring, so he paid my apprenticeship fees and bought me a sewing machine and other materials. However, my tailoring business has not gone well. I want to be financially comfortable one day so I can support my children, especially Gbenga, who is musically talented. In appearance, he is identical to his father, but his father has no interest in him. It is left to me to help him, which I am not capable of doing. Nikẹ advised me to return to artwork. Nikẹ is someone I cannot forget. She is a friend to me indeed. She tries to lift my head from poverty. I need money to buy materials, and there is the problem of finding a market for my work. Nikẹ is the reason I am where I am today. She gave me money for supplies and other materials that are scarce.

I am always sad. I have many responsibilities: four children from each husband, and I am the one who must struggle with them. I am the type of woman who gets pregnant anytime I have intercourse with my husband. And during this time I knew nothing of family planning.[15] It was not until I had my last child that I told the doctor that I did not want anymore. That is when I learned about family planning.[16]

My second husband lost his job as a public servant, so the financial load is on me. I find it difficult to cope with it all. I don't know exactly what causes me to have these problems; maybe it is the low standard of my education and marrying too early in life. Part of the problem is polygyny, though. It is better to have a one man—one wife system. I have an uncle whose wife is a Roman Catholic. They are mono-gamous. They have worked hand-in-hand to care for their children. Some of their children are studying abroad. In a polygynous system the wives fight among themselves for supremacy. This fighting has caused me to be in the situation I am in now.

If I could change anything about my society I would put an end to bride-price. The use of bride-price involves selling a woman, and the husband uses the fact that he paid money for his wife as an excuse to mistreat her. I am not concerned about collecting bride-price for my daughters. I do not want men abusing them. Other things I would change about our traditions include anything that affects human feel-ings or engenders conflict in families or between ethnic groups. One example is the washing of the bride's feet. Sometimes after the bride's legs are washed, sores appear. That is the work of wicked people who place charms in the water. I would stop the replaiting of hair and the changing of clothes. The woman who replaits the new wife's hair might put a charm in the new wife's hair that causes her to become insane. I would halt the giving of the placenta to the husband after a child is born.[17] If the husband is not around, the afterbirth is given to a senior wife. But the senior wife might be unhappy with the new wife. She might cook the placenta in the mother's food, resulting in the mother's illness. When I was young I witnessed so many things. The placenta should be destroyed with chemicals and washed away.

I left my current husband's house because of the jealousy of the co-wives. When I arrived he had only one wife. She and I cooked together and got along. He would give the senior wife housekeeping money. She would take some and give the remainder to me to buy food. When the third wife came, he gave each of us money separately, and we prepared our own food. In order to provoke me, the wives would talk and sing songs against me whenever my husband and I held private conversations. They believed I was his favorite. In fact, he did love me, because whenever I was sad he would talk to me and stay with me. I became quite ill during my first pregnancy with my second husband. I was vomiting blood. I had never had a difficult pregnancy before, so my illness had to be the work of my enemies. I went to my father and told him the situation. I suspected my co-wives of using charms against me. My father cut incisions on my chest for protection. I studied the situation and felt it best to live alone. Although my husband felt sad, I told him that, at my age, I had to settle down and plan for the future. He is free to come and visit me anytime, but as soon as he no longer approves of my living alone he can just divorce me.[18]

I have found that I like living alone. I feel fine and free. If I want to go out, there is no one who will quarrel with me. If I want to relax, no one tells me to go and cook. Because I am now doing artwork, I need time.[19] To be an artist you must think deeply and sketch figures. There were times in my second marriage that I was thinking about my work and the junior wife would begin giving me problems. This drew my attention away from what I was doing. In staying alone I have a lot of time to concentrate on my work. It is good for a woman to live like this, especially if she has problems. Alone, she can plan her life. She can reason and think without interruption. No one can harass her when she is relaxing.

# Notes

## Introduction (pages xv–xlii)

1. Mbari Mbayo of Oṣogbo was an artists' group established by the late Duro Ladipọ, an actor, composer, as well as producer and director of the Duro Ladipọ National Theater. Ladipọ turned his hostel and pub into a theater and gallery. Mbari Mbayo nurtured the talent of writers, performers, and visual artists through workshop rather than art school methods (Kennedy 1968).

2. Carroll Parrott Blue's film, *Nigerian Art—Kindred Spirits*, was coproduced by television station WETA, Washington, D.C. and the Smithsonian Institution. Funding was received from the Southwestern Bell Corporation. It was first aired on March 5, 1990, and was featured as "a look at modern Nigerian art through the eyes of the artists who create it," namely, El Anatusi, Nikẹ Davies, Sokari Douglas Camp, Ben Enwonwu, Lamidi Fakẹyẹ, Emmanuel Taiwo, Nkiru Nzegwu, and Uche Okeke.

3. All the cotton Ibitọla used came from the farm as raw material. She removed the seeds and hand spun the cotton. Thus, it was possible to produce only two small *ọjas* daily. (For a detailed account of hand processing see Eicher 1976, pp. 13–20.)

4. In the article "Adirẹ Art" by Stephen Mugambi, in the May 1992 issue of the Kenyan magazine *Rainbow,* Davies gave a detailed and extensive explanation of the process of making *adirẹ*. I quote her in full to convey to the reader how labor-intensive this process is. There are four major raw materials used to make *adirẹ*: cloth, cassava tubers to make starch, cocoa shells, and indigo dye.

First I collect many young leaves of the indigo plant. . . .then I pound them. I store the pounded leaves of the indigo plant in a container while I prepare the other raw materials.

Cocoa shells are the outer covers of cocoa beans. . . . They are left behind as a waste product when the cocoa bean is removed to make cocoa and chocolate. I take dry cocoa shells and set them on fire. I collect the ash that is produced and dissolve it in water.

I remove anything that does not dissolve by pouring the mixture through a piece of cloth. I collect the solution that passes through the cloth in a container. Then I mix it with powdered indigo plant leaves.

Chemicals from the ash will help fix the dye onto the cloth. They make it permanent.

The dye mixture is put in a pot and left in the sun for about seven days. The dye is ready for use when the mixture turns yellow. If something has gone wrong, the mixture turns black. . . .

*Adire* artists use cassava tubers to make a paste. The paste is used to paint patterns on the cloth. The cloth is dipped into the indigo dye . . . areas that are covered with cassava paste do not pick up dye.

The cassava tubers are first peeled and then soaked in water for about a week. . . . They are then squeezed by hand to remove a poisonous chemical that is normally found in cassava.

Tubers are broken into small pieces and dried in the sun. . . . The dry pieces are ground into a powder, which is boiled in water.

A small amount of chemical called alum is added to the mixture. . . . Alum is normally used to fix dyes in the textile industry. In making *adire,* it gives a light blue colour to the patterns.

After boiling, the mixture is squeezed through a fine cloth such as chiffon or muslin. What comes through the cloth is collected. It provides the paste for drawing the beautiful designs.

A chicken feather is used to apply cassava paste onto the cloth to make patterns. . . .

The cloth is dipped into the indigo dye to pick up colour.

When the cloth is taken out, it looks yellow. However, in two or three minutes, it changes colour to indigo. The places that are covered in paste are very pale blue. The cloth is then dried.

The process is repeated about ten times. This is done to colour the fabric as deeply as possible.

The fabric is soaked in water overnight to remove the cassava paste. Then it is washed in water containing some vinegar.

The vinegar helps the cloth not to lose too much colour. . . . Traditionally, a piece of wood was used to beat an *adire* to make it shine. . . .

Sometimes I use modern textile dyes in different colours. I use pieces of plastic foam instead of chicken feathers, and candle wax instead of cassava paste (pp. 12–13).

The use of candle wax and colored dyes is generally called batik; the term *adire* still refers to the blue and white indigo-dyed cloth.

5. Helen Ware's (1979) study of married Yoruba women's views on polygyny revealed that "so strong are the social pressures to accept the practice, that most women claimed to be happy to welcome a new co-wife even when their responses

showed them to hate the thought" (p. 188). When asked to name the good things about being married to a man with several wives, 22 percent of the women said there were none, 25 percent named one advantage, 43 percent named two (namely, help with housework and the division of labor), and only 10 percent could think of three advantages. Asked about the bad things, 85 percent of the women responded in terms of envy, jealousy, murder, hatred, chaos, and devilishness. The jealousy stems less from sexual rivalry, than from women's attempts at securing limited economic resources. (That women divorce their husbands seldom because of men's infidelities, but more frequently because the men financially neglect the wives or their children [Lloyd 1968] is an indication that sexual jealousy does not figure as significantly as does competition for material resources.) Ware reported that women prefer that their husbands have co-wives rather than mistresses because the men spend more on mistresses. Also, women were unlikely to limit their childbearing, as this would also limit their share of the husband's resources. The only circumstances under which the women might limit childbearing was if other wives also agreed to do so or if a woman had negotiated with her husband for the educational needs of her existing children. Almost half of the women respondents (47 percent) in the Ware study stated that, aside from having children, women do not need husbands. They felt that women were equal to men; given many of the disadvantages of marriage, women were better off on their own. For those who thought husbands were valuable, 16 percent felt that their value lay in companionship; other functions of the husband included advice (11 percent), working together (10 percent), and sexual satisfaction (2 percent). A mere 7 percent felt that women needed to have husbands for economic support.

Although sexual jealousy does not result in divorce, that does not mean that women do not often find it painful to have a sexual rival. One polygynist, Isaac Olu Oyewumi, took a third and much younger wife in comparison to his first two. The older wives no longer wanted to have children, and both were sleeping with him less and less. The young wife, jealous of the fertility of the older two, began using "love potions" to monopolize the husband. She put love potions in his bathwater, in food she cooked for him, and in a shell under his pillow. When Oyewumi's son had an extramarital affair that resulted in his mistress's pregnancy, Oyewumi forced his son to marry her. The son's first wife was so angry that she accused the new bride of witchcraft, having planted the "charms" herself. Both "offending" junior wives were threatened with divorce (Plotnicov 1967).

6. *Gari* and *akara* balls are very inexpensive food staples that can be bought along the road throughout southwestern Nigeria.

7. Nigerian women have long been interested in forming their own dramatic groups. For example, in the 1930s, Ọlaniwun Adunni Oluwọle, who routinely won prominent roles in plays organized by the Girl's Guild of St. John's Church in Lagos, broke out of the confines of the guild to organize her own play. The play was directed by Nigerian nationalist Herbert Macaulay and was very successful. Oluwọle's tremendous leadership ability led her to become a leading political figure, and she was one of the first women to form a political party (Olusanya 1992).

8. I do not mention Davies's husband by name for reasons discussed below in an introductory section entitled "Origin of the Study."

9. For a discussion of women's exclusion from Nigerian history as an aca-

demic discipline see Bọllanle Awẹ's (1991) article "Writing Women into History: The Nigerian Experience."

10. In the Smithsonian World's documentary *Nigerian Art—Kindred Spirits*, Davies is featured together with Sokari Douglas Camp and several male artists. Camp has broken many traditional gender barriers by creating sculpture, working in metal, and orchestrating simulated Kalabari Ijo spirit masquerades as Kalabari women would have perceived them (Aronson 1991). Like Davies, Camp had to "move far away from her Kalabari environment in order to become a successful contemporary artist" (p. 573). Camp studied and married in England (Aronson 1991).

11. We see from Aronson's (1978) profile of a Yoruba woman, Alice Bankọle, the important role of this deity in women's lives. Bankọle consulted Ọṣun when her only daughter, just a year old, was taken ill; everyone thought she was going to die. The priestesses gave Bankọle's daughter water to drink from the Ọṣun River, and the child recovered immediately. Ọṣun was consulted on two more occasions: once when her daughter had a boil on her back and then when her daughter had neck pains. In neither case could Ibadan doctors cure the malady. When her daughter became ill during her pregnancy, Bankọle again consulted Ọṣun. Although her daughter was in the hospital, Bankọle brought gifts to the Ọṣun worshipers. Her daughter recovered and delivered the baby, who in turn became ill. Bankọle believed the baby became ill because she had not brought the baby to the shrine as she had been asked to do. Bankọle went to the shrine, and when she returned to Ibadan the baby was well.

12. Davies was thinking of a Yoruba proverb that warns against speaking the name of one's enemy. I was thinking of Mr. —— from Alice Walker's (1982) *The Color Purple,* and we delighted in this approach. It resolved several issues with respect to Davies's own goals of autonomy and her aim to use her life to demonstrate and keep attention focused on women's difficulties in polygynous marriages.

13. Rachel Agheyisi (1985) wrote that a girl's selection of a particular type of educational training is heavily influenced by parents and peers, whose views in turn reflect social attitudes regarding a woman's place. The decision, made early in life, closes the door to many career opportunities and directs the girl to socially approved female segments of the labor market. As a result of unequal educational opportunities (with parents preferring to educate boys, not girls) and gender role socialization, in addition to direct and indirect discrimination in the labor market, the percentage of women in the modern sector is very low. Agheyisi estimates women's employment in this sector to be around 20 percent.

14. Nigerians refer to the bride-price as dowry. The bride-price is paid to the woman's family by the fiancé and consists of money, symbolic tokens, and gifts for the bride and her family. If the bride-price is not paid, a customary marriage has not taken place. As Davies's father never accepted a bride-price for her from the artist, she was not a wife in the strict traditional sense. Because she observed all the formalities and carried out the obligations of a married woman, however, she considered herself married, as did all of Oṣogbo.

15. Davies's strategies for negotiating patriarchy are well honed and can be thought of in terms of "trickster strategies." J. W. Roberts (1989) wrote that Africans place a high value on native intelligence in handling situations stemming

from social repression and material shortage that place the individual at a disadvantage. Those in positions of formal power can get their needs met and desires fulfilled by virtue of their office, in socially and religiously sanctioned ways. Those at the bottom of the hierarchy rely on wit and clever cheating to survive.

Cleverness is a valuable adaptive behavioral trait when it is undertaken in a manner that does not threaten the well-being of the group (Roberts 1989). During her married life, Davies allowed her husband to "take her for a dummy" on the occasions when she would loan him money or approach women he wanted to marry. That Davies only helped to enrich the lives of the co-wives is a clear indication that her strategies did not threaten them. I asked the first and second co-wives if they were jealous of Davies's early success. On the contrary, because of Davies's character the women cared for her deeply. They were not jealous of her, as she always took their works to sell, drove her co-wives around in her car, and fed their children. As of 1988, these two former co-wives had laid the foundations for their own houses on either side of Davies's first studio/gallery.

Davies was able to make her husband believe that she was a grateful partner in his family, and while, as Roberts wrote, the trickster seemed to participate in the illusion of cooperation, she was ever mindful of the politics of the compound where she learned and mastered (with the help especially of her fifth co-wife) the treacherous ways of their husband. While dealing with these ways daily, she learned not to share in the illusion of a shared identity with her husband. The wives' discussion about their husband telling each wife in private that he loved her more than the others and that she, therefore, was the owner of their house was the beginning of Davies's understanding of this illusion (see pages 56–57.) Ama Ata Aidoo (1984) has written, based on her own experiences as a woman in African higher education, that "clarity therefore becomes the only reliable companion and weapon for a fighting woman. For with such company and thus armed, she can weather sexist disillusion and betrayal, and still move on" (p. 264).

16. Fertility and family planning surveys may underestimate infant mortality rates since children who die are omitted from a birth history either through oversight or because people are unwilling to talk about them (Entwisle and Coles 1990). Though infant mortality rates have been declining, as late as 1968, Peter Lloyd (1968) noted that 50 percent of Yoruba children died before the age of five. Maclean (1982) suggests that the concept of the *abiku* is an explanation for the epidemic levels of infant mortality. *Abiku* children (those born to die) live with their parents for a while and then die, only to return again. Mothers call their *abiku* children by special names, such as "stay and bury me," and treat them indulgently in the hope that they will remain.

17. Cross-dressing and transvestism are common during rituals and not unheard of during public festivals and annual ceremonies to various deities such as Agẹmọ, Ṣango, and Eṣu. Agẹmọ priests wear their hair plaited in female style. Priests of Ṣango also wear women's hairstyles. A priestess possessed by Eṣu may wear a carved penis and testicles under her skirt. During possession, individuals actually undergo gender transformation. Iya Ṣango, a priestess of Ṣango, becomes Ṣango, and even in her daily life she has access to this deity's masculine power. At public festivals, daughters may wear their fathers' clothes so they can dash about more aggressively. A man may give a woman who is dancing with large forceful gestures his outer garment to make the dance "look fine" (Drewal 1992).

Theatrical cross-dressing is also common. Funmilayọ Ranko often dresses in male costumes on stage and as of 1984 was one of only two women who headed her own traveling theater troupe (Jeyifọ 1984).

18. According to Adefioye Oyeṣakin (1987), Yoruba society categorizes women who are talented intellectually or physically or both as men disguised as women. In traditional poetry women are often portrayed as inefficient in most human endeavors.

19. For a general overview of Nigerian women's roles as mothers, wives, and workers derived from fertility and family planning survey data, see Barbara Entwisle and Catherine Coles's (1990) "Demographic Surveys and Nigerian Women." For an overview of new government policies directed at improving the condition of Nigerian women through "gender-specific" and existing development programs, see Simi Afọnja's (1989) "Toward the Creation of a New Order for Nigerian Women: Recent Trends in Politics and Policies."

## Chapter 1 (pages 3–15)

1. *Gari* is derived from cassava that has been peeled, washed, and grated on a metal pan in which holes have been punched. "The gratings are put into a cotton bag which is placed on a stool or some other object to keep it off the ground. A heavy weight is placed on the bag, which is allowed to drain under pressure for from two to four days. It is then sifted and toasted" (Bascom 1951b, p. 127). A small amount of *gari* is mixed with boiling water. It is often a morning drink and the only food many take before lunch.

2. According to Margaret Drewal (1992), the corpse is washed in a preparation of herbs, water, and sacrificial blood from goats by a member of the Oṣugbo society (society of elders that formed the judiciary of the community). The eldest living child rubs chalk and camwood into the palms of the parent to signify that the child is assisting the parent into the otherworld, just as the parent once assisted the child's entry into this one.

3. "Wrapping the corpse of the wise elder" occurs when relatives and friends bring cloth for the Oṣugbo members to wrap around the body. The volume of the cloth indicates the social significance of the deceased (Drewal 1992).

4. Wọle Ṣoyinka (1988) offered a similar description of the material possessions of his aunts who worked as itinerant traders. These women trekked forty miles from their village, Iṣara, to Ake carrying their heavy loads every market day. Ṣoyinka noted their poverty. "Beneath their joy at our presence we now sensed the strain of sheer survival. . . . Their one dress of pride was worn in our honor whenever they came to take us out, and the same dress would appear again at the most important festival of the year, the New Year itself, then disappear . . . until the next festival" (p. 130).

5. The Yoruba diet is high in starch. Of the fifty-six recipes W. R. Bascom (1951a) collected in one city (Ifẹ), forty-seven consisted of various ways to prepare yam, maize, plantain, cassava, or coco yam. Leafy vegetables are used in the preparation of stews and fruits; though these are numerous, they are not that important in the diet.

6. Sandra Barnes (1990) noted that marital relationships are most important

for women between the ages of twenty and thirty, primarily due to their childbearing capacities. Middle-aged women move from roles stressing reproduction and parenting to roles emphasizing grandparenting and caring for their older relatives. Older woman are "considered undesirable conjugal partners and frequently are labeled as 'used cargo' " (p. 259). Throughout their lives, men maintain their conjugal relationships to the same woman or to younger wives by either serial monogamy or polygyny. Thus, they have access to the sexual and domestic services of women well into old age.

7. According to Bascom (1951a), meat was a food for ceremonies and special occasions. Most Yoruba ate meat when an animal died or when one was sacrificed. Only chiefs and wealthy people could afford to buy meat in the market or kill a domestic animal. Even well into the 1950s, meat in stews was considered the food of the well-to-do. Thus, "stealing meat from a soup-pot was considered particularly heinous. . . . If the thief, when caught, had already swallowed the evidence of his crime, he was made to carry the soup-pot on his head, and his mouth was smeared with oil from the pot" (Ṣoyinka 1988, p. 89).

8. A special group of Yoruba women traders, *alaseta onję*, cook food for sale in the market, street corners, and various other high-traffic spots such as along highways. These serve the purpose of restaurants. Foods available include pounded yam, boiled yam, plantain, stew, steamed beans, and rice (Bascom 1951a).

9. Any large leaves that did not flavor the food were used. Common leaves included banana leaves and other leaves used also for thatching roofs (Bascom 1951b).

10. *Talla*, or street hawking of cooked food, was commonly practiced by young girls in the North. They used their profits for furniture and other goods they wished to bring to their marital home (Schildkrout 1987). Unlike that of Hausa girls, Davies's hawking was not to secure her trousseau but to contribute to the household economy.

11. There were many Yoruba settled in Jos, a significant number of whom lived in a section of town called Issele Ifę (the descendants of Ifę) (Plotnicov 1967). Ile-Ifę is the preeminent religious and historical site of the Yoruba. The mythology holds that the deity Oduduwa descended from heaven to form earth at this site. The sons of Oduduwa moved from the city to form other kingdoms, and hence major Yoruba rulers trace their descent from Oduduwa (Eades 1980).

12. The types of female genital mutilation include (a) circumcision, a procedure in which the prepuce, or hood, of the clitoris is cut away; (b) excision, a method by which the clitoris is cut and all or a part of the labia minora is removed; (c) intermediate, wherein the same organs are removed as in excision as well as the removal of parts of the labia majora as desired by family members; and (d) infibulation, which incorporates all of the intermediate followed by the sewing of the two sides of the vulva together with silk or catgut sutures. A small opening for the passage of menstrual blood or urine is made possible by the insertion of a tiny piece of wood or reed (Dorkenoo and Elworthy 1992).

13. Female genital mutilation is now being defined as a violation of human rights by a diverse group of organizations, including the London-based Minority Rights Group (MRG). According to Article 5 of the Universal Declaration of Human Rights, no one should be subjected to torture or cruel, inhuman, or de-

grading treatment. The MRG maintains that female genital mutilation is a violation of children's rights as well because, unlike adults, who can freely submit to ritual practices, children do not have informed judgment. Female children do "not consent but simply under[go] the operation (which in this case is irrevocable) while [they are] totally vulnerable. The descriptions available of the reactions of children—panic and shock from extreme pain, convulsions, necessity for six adults to hold down an eight-year-old, and death—indicate a practice comparable to torture" (Dorkenoo and Elworthy 1992, p. 16). It is torture inflicted in the name not of political conviction or military necessity but of tradition. Due to the short- and long-term medical complications of this mutilation, the practice is viewed as a violation of children's rights to good psychological and physical health (Dorkenoo and Elworthy 1992). Davies opposes the perpetuation of female genital mutilation for these reasons.

14. Clitoridectomy was traditionally performed during the betrothal period after a young man and his family completed the *idana* (bride-price; called "dowry" in Nigerian English). The *idana* consisted of a money payment, symbolic presents, consultation of the Ifa oracle, and a feast for the man's fiancée. The young woman underwent the procedure; she also received three long vertical stripes on her right foreleg and three on her left forearm. The family of the husband-to-be then sent the "load" for the bride; palm oil and breadstuffs for the wound, food for her forced confinement, as well as firewood. A female or male circumciser performed the surgery. No special prayers or religious rituals accompanied the procedure. The young woman's mother or mother-in-law, or a postmenopausal woman, dressed her wounds, and her fiancée's sisters stayed with her throughout her one-month confinement. When she emerged from confinement she had put on weight; this was a signal to the fiancée to set the date for the bride to come to his family's home (Fadipẹ 1970). Among certain groups of Yoruba, a girl could undergo clitoridectomy any time before her tenth birthday (Dennett 1910/1968) or as early as eight days old (Talbot 1926/1969).

15. The age of marriage for Yoruba girls is between seventeen and twenty-five. At the turn of the century, girls were betrothed at birth, not infrequently to friends of their fathers. Since that time the period between engagement and consummation of the marriage has been shortened (Eades 1980). A 1973 survey of more than six thousand Yoruba women residing in Ibadan revealed that 63 percent of the fifteen- to nineteen-year-olds were not married (Ware 1979).

16. The MRG suggests that female genital mutilation persists because marriage for many women constitutes a primary means of survival. In societies where excision is a prerequisite for marriage, women are unlikely to allow their daughters to forgo the practice. Development analysts speculate that development projects that assist women in gaining access to education and economic resources will encourage them to let go of certain traditional practices as survival mechanisms in times of socioeconomic change (Dorkenoo and Elworthy 1992).

The Hosken Report (1982) estimates that about half of all Nigerian women have undergone genital mutilation. Nigerian journalist Esther Ogunmọdẹde, who also has undergone the procedure, has spearheaded the campaign to eradicate the practice by calling attention to the medical problems associated with it. She found that all groups in Nigeria practice mutilation, which means that it cuts across linguistic and religious differences. She has called for the education of the populace through various institutions such as maternity clinics, women's societies, schools and colleges, hospitals, and nursing and medical schools. She believes that legislative efforts would simply drive the practice underground. Alternative income sources for circumcisers is not needed since there are a small number of such professionals (estimated at one per three thousand), and they perform male circumcisions in addition to their occupations as barbers, traditional healers, farmers, or traders (Dorkenoo and Elworthy 1992). Traditionally, payment to a circumciser consists of a very small amount of money, a yam, a snail, a bottle of palm oil, and kola nuts (Uka 1966).

17. The belief among the Yoruba that a newborn child would die if its head touched the clitoris during delivery was noted by participant observers in a 1966 study by Ngwobia Uka. The Yoruba traditionally believed that an uncircumcised woman was a promiscuous individual. Any children she had were thought to have been conceived in lust and therefore outside ritually sanctioned marriage. The clitoris is known euphemistically as "the king inside the world" and its removal seems to be a preparation for a woman's role as wife and mother of children of the patrilineage (Matory 1994). Drawing on spirit possession and marriage symbolism, Matory (1994) suggests that female bodily vessels must be emptied and refilled with the will or inner "head" of the god or patrilineage. When the clitoris is not removed a woman cannot serve as a vessel for the patrilineage. Since the child shares the inner "head" or identity of the patrilineal ancestors, Matory believes that the linking of the maternal king (the clitoris) with the child's head signals a social, rather than an actual, death for the infant of an uncircumcised mother.

18. The elaborate funeral ceremony is carried out by a society or association to which the deceased belonged.

19. Margaret Drewal (1992) found that the interment of the corpse is a preliminary activity to the funeral proper. The performances are decided on by the family, and it is these that complete the funeral. The performances may take place anywhere from a month to a year or more after the burial. This gives the family time to accumulate resources. Drewal described a program of seven days in which the first or main day is the ritual; the third day is for feasting; the fourth day is for public celebration; and the seventh is a final celebration day. The play, feasting, and celebration are part of the sacrifice to the deceased.

20. Sandra Barnes (1990) found that women migrants in urban areas cannot automatically depend on kin in their hometown as a source of security as they grow older. "Time erases memories and estranges kinsmen and kinswomen from one another" (p. 258). Individuals have to work to maintain these ties—through gift giving, fostering hometown children, or offering hospitality to family when they visit the city. To meet their kinship obligations, women must be economically successful in the midst of conditions where they do not have the support of their kin, that is, in a distant community. Unsuccessful women find it difficult to ask for help. Although no one is rejected, the reception for the poor is lukewarm.

21. "Reddish women are often praised by African men; and African women use red camwood as a cosmetic" (Gleason 1992, p. 182). See also Eve de Negri (1976) for a description of women's use of red camwood for various ceremonial occasions.

22. According to Bascom (1951a), coco yams are substituted for yams by the

poor. They are prepared as a loaf (i.e., through pounding) and eaten with stews or mixed with yams, cassava, plantains, or bananas to vary the flavor.

23. Palm oil comes from the fibrous flesh that lies outside the shell of the palmnut. This oil is reddish orange and is different from palm-kernel oil, a white oil used in soap (Bascom 1951a).

24. Bascom (1951a) noted that the food of unmarried men was usually prepared by a female relative or a woman living in his compound; otherwise the man bought cooked food in the market. Ridicule and gossip were directed at a man who cooked his own food. Such men are considered either miserly or so wicked that female relatives do not want to bother with them. The simple question "Why are you cooking?" is taken to be an insult. A man staying at his farm, however, can cook for himself without criticism.

25. It was the role of certain *Egungun* (masked individuals who were thought to represent ancestral spirits) to admonish women. Egungun Agan, for example, was the executor of women accused of witchcraft and of those proved guilty of crimes such as murder and incendiarism (Johnson 1921/1969, p. 29).

## Chapter 2 (pages 16–26)

1. The principal inheritors of a woman's property were her siblings. The woman's children inherited what was left after the siblings had satisfied themselves. The siblings had an obligation to care for the dependent children of the deceased, however. Half-brothers and half-sisters and their children had as much right to the property of the deceased as did the deceased's own children. Also, those who contributed to the funeral ceremonies of the deceased were permitted an inheritance. Men did not inherit from their wives, and older relatives did not inherit the property of younger ones nor did they take part in funeral ceremonies, save to receive condolences (Fadipẹ 1970).

2. The research assistants in Uka's (1966) study reported cases in which girls burst into tears and were very frightened by their first periods. It was only then that mothers discussed with girls the meaning of the period. About 60 percent of their sample indicated that the onset of menarche is age thirteen.

## Chapter 3 (pages 27–38)

1. Christine Obbo (1980) found that rural women migrate to towns because of limited resources and personal dissatisfaction. Individuals leave the village to escape their inferior positions in the socioeconomic village system. One's place in the strata is determined by numerous factors, such as age, sibling order, and having few family ties in the rural community, which is often the case for an unmarried member of a small family. Women migrate for various reasons, including to be with their husbands, to follow boyfriends who have excited them with their descriptions of town life, to get away from unsatisfactory marriages, and to seek a job or their "fortune."

2. After interviewing *babalawos*, Raymond Prince (1964) found that "the practice of sorcery often involves the use of human body parts—skulls, bones,

limbs, organs, and so forth. It is difficult to know how frequent the practice is, but it is the unanimous opinion of the healers that it is extremely common. Indeed, one often sees in the local press accounts of murders committed to obtain body parts for 'medicine' or descriptions of the discovered of mutilated corpses that have presumably been used for the same purposes" (p. 89). The alleged use of money-making magic in which people's heads are used to carry a calabash that issues forth money after incantations and other magical rituals have been performed is called "*lukudi.*" The victim is murdered and the body supposedly is kept (Matory, 1994).

3. Afro-beat was pioneered by Fẹla Anikulapo-Kuti. Afro-beat combines African dance band highlife (a term for Anglophone West African popular music), jazz, and African American dance music of the 1960s. It appealed to a wide cross-section of cosmopolitan and street-wise youths including urban migrants, wage workers, and college students. The lyrics of the music stress political inequalities, such as neo-colonialism, and are sung in pidgin English (Waterman 1990). Christopher Waterman (1990) suggests that it is a less popular form of music because of Fẹla's "deviant public image: he *shaks* (smokes marijuana), takes advantage of young migrant women from the village, defies constituted authority, and engages in explicit abusive language (*yabis*)" (p. 227). During our interviews, Davies often discussed Fẹla's well-known polygynous setup as an injustice to women.

4. In 1966, bride-price in Yorubaland varied between 12 and 30 pounds (Uka 1966), or 24 to 60 niara.

5. Negative events (e.g., an illness or inexplicable death of a loved one) in one's life are usually attributed to witchcraft, but magic is often evoked to explain why an individual followed a certain course of action. For example, Christopher Waterman (1990) reported on a musician, Tunde King, who returned to Lagos after an eleven-year absence. King attributed this to a jealous competitor who nailed an *oogun*, that is, a magical power object, to the dock from which he embarked. "The oogun caused him to forget his home, despite many letters from friends and admirers in Lagos. When the nail disintegrated and the power object sank beneath the waves, King came home" (p. 76).

## Chapter 4 (pages 39–48)

1. This is certainly a shared sentiment among African women. Awusara, a Ghanian woman, once narrated a tale of a python who turned himself into a man. As a man, he wooed a young woman and convinced her to marry him. Once in their hut, he began to devour the woman. When asked by a male listener about the meaning of the story, a woman replied: "As the man wants to marry a woman, he will keep on deceiving her until she's convinced, and as soon as they marry, the man will show his true character." When the male listener asked if the woman was foolish for marrying the python, the woman exclaimed: "Not at all! When a man woos a girl, he tells her sweet words. After marrying her, the man changes" (Fikry-Atallah 1972, p. 407).

2. A *ṣigidi* is an image made of mud and is believed to have the power of protecting, avenging, and attacking when propitiated (Ṣowande 1991). Oyesakin

(1987) described it as a human shape molded from clay. When imbued with magical properties, it can go on an errand of destruction.

3. Alhaji Shehu Shagari, president of Nigeria from 1979 to 1983.

## Chapter 5 (pages 49–54)

1. The Christ Apostolic Church banned the use of all medicines, traditional or western (Eades 1980). According to Davies's former senior wife, the drinking of holy water made her feel powerful, and, thus, delivery without medicine was possible.

2. During the naming ceremony, prayers are offered for the child. Foods are placed on the child's lips. People place money into a basin or calabash half-filled with water that is in front of the child. The guests are entertained for the rest of the day. In the past, the Ifa priest would perform a divination to determine the child's names and sacrifice a cock on behalf of the child to the appropriate ancestors and deities (Uka 1966).

3. The Yoruba gave children four names: One indicates the conditions under which the baby was born. For example, *Iyamide* indicates that the child is a reincarnation of a grandmother. The second name is the christening name and is given to girls on the sixth day after birth and to boys on the eighth day. The *oriki* is the third name and conveys the positive qualities the relatives hope the child will have. One such name is *Agbaje*, which means "the conqueror in struggle." The fourth name is the one shared by all the family members (Uka 1966).

4. Spreading a cloth on which money is placed is a long-standing tradition (Drewal 1992).

5. Maclean (1982) found that when infants die, mothers bewail in "wild abandoned weeping, their untimely demise, which is less noisily grieved by the males in the family" (p. 171), but general adult mourning is not occasioned.

6. Ware (1979) reported that it is widely believed that co-wife-inspired witchcraft constitutes a major factor in infant death.

7. Ifa is thought to have the answers to all human problems. Ifa is consulted for any important decisions and to resolve conflicts and solve problems. The priest of Ifa is called a *babalawo*. *Awo* stands for secrets, and *baba* means father, so the term refers to father of secrets (Abimbọla 1975). Since the priesthood of Ifa is a religious one, the *babalawos* regularly refer clients to join one of the many cults as revealed through the divination process (Bascom 1941).

## Chapter 6 (pages 55–64)

1. Fadipẹ (1970) reported that if the bride is "found" not to be a virgin, the husband physically assaults the bride to determine the identity of the despoiler. When the culprit is identified, the husband then "sues for damages" the man or men who "deflowered" his bride. A symbol of the bride's "unchaste" state is sent to her family. These symbols vary in form and consist of, for example, a calabash gourd half-filled with palm wine or cowry shells in which holes have been punched. The rough treatment of women does not stop there. The two female relatives or age-mates who are stationed outside the room where the consumma-

tion is taking place then flee. There have been cases in which the husband beat up the bride's associates, causing permanent physical damage. Fadipe noted that the bride's associates, upon determination of the bride's non-virginal state, leave the relative safety of the husband's compound and run back to their village or home in spite of the danger to those "of their sex" when out on the road at night. The bride might be flogged by her father to determine the identity of the man she slept with (or, possibly, who coerced her). Although the husband does not divorce her, the new wife would not receive the full amount of presents from her husband's kin, and she suffers a loss of face. Moreover, her co-wives may taunt her with the discovery during arguments. The bride who is a virgin, as evidenced by blood from the ruptured hymen spread on a white cloth, is the cause of celebration. The cloth, money, and a hen for sacrifice might be sent to the wife's family that night, and the husband, accompanied by drummers and associates, visits the bride's parents to thank them.

2. Davies uses the word "voodoo" to refer to the negative practices associated with sorcery and to the medicines that had sleep-inducing effects.

3. Seniority is not derived from age. A man's first wife may be younger in age than his second or third, but the first wife is senior to those he marries after her. With seniority comes increased status, as junior wives do most of the domestic work (Bascom 1942).

## Chapter 7 (pages 65–75)

1. Victoria Scott, an artist and art historian, wrote an article describing Davies's embroidery and batiks that appeared in *African Art* (1983). Scott also organized exhibitions for both Davies and her brother, Joseph Ọlabọde, at the Stewart Gallery in Dallas, Texas; the Denton Unitarian Fellowship Hall in Denton, Texas; the Malcolm Brown Gallery in Cleveland, Ohio; and workshops in the American Southwest. Scott was pivotal in Davies's participation in the Edinburgh Festival in Scotland, an exhibition of Oṣogbo artists (Staff 1985a).

2. The Aladura churches developed from factions or praying bands within the missionary churches who organized themselves as a special unit for the specific purpose of meeting the everyday needs of Yoruba Christians. The missionary religions were perceived as concerned more with salvation in the next world than with solving problems within this one; namely, healing, and providing knowledge of the future and protection against witchcraft. The Aladura prophet, pastor, or preacher interprets dreams and visions and operates in ways similar to *babalawos*. When the missionary authorities deemed these practices unorthodox, the praying bands broke away. By 1958, a praying band named the Christ Apostolic Church (CAC) had become the third-largest church in western Nigeria. Within the CAC, the Bible is seen as the ultimate spiritual authority, yet aspects of the Yoruba worldview are prominent. First, words are considered to have power to bring about desired conditions in the physical world. In addition, charms are prepared that include verses from the Bible; holy water is extensively used; and pilgrimages to sacred hills (reminiscent of hill festivals in traditional religion) are annual events. Drumming and dancing are an especially important part of religious worship (Eades 1980).

3. According to Eades (1980), the Christ Apostolic Church bans polygyny, and this might account in part for this prediction.

4. Obbo (1975) presents the case study of a migrant woman in Uganda whose husband was unaware of her status as a homeowner. This woman, Fatuma, sold cooked food, brewed gin, and had two influential boyfriends who gave her gifts. She built a house with ten rooms to rent out. She reported only a meager amount of her monthly earnings to her husband.

## Chapter 8 (pages 76–80)

1. For a detailed case study of factionalism in Yoruba markets over the course of nine years, see Sandra Barnes's (1986) "Factionalism in Yoruba Markets." These factions start out as rivalries between women leaders for control of key positions within market association hierarchies, often with an eye toward gaining positions on various political councils. Over time these factions spread to include the larger community as the leaders garner support from local leaders, male and female, and with various attempts to sway public opinion. Such women market leaders are and usually remain "rivals for life."

2. Each Yoruba rural market is part of a "ring." The entire ring consists of series of day or night markets that occur at regular intervals of four days or multiples of four-day intervals (Hodder 1962). Each market in the ring takes place on successive days; thus, no two markets in a ring occur on the same day. The exact location of the market shifts from day to day but is always within comfortable walking distance (of several miles) of the villages the ring serves. Hodder estimated that a woman usually attends at least two of these markets in an eight-day cycle and conveys by headload (up to about eighty pounds) the wares she will sell. The days on which markets occur are referred to as "market days," and very little trading takes place on nonmarket days. For rural markets, as many as three thousand to four thousand people (mainly women) attend. The primary economic activity is the small-scale individual buying and selling of products in very modest quantities.

3. This sixteenth-century ruler of the Hausa state Zazzau is remembered for her prowess as a military leader and expansionist (Abubakr 1992).

4. Aniwura was born in the mid- to late 1820s. Her wealth was derived from the tobacco trade. Those she enslaved (more than two hundred individuals) increased her wealth substantially, as many women wove a durable cloth that was in demand locally and in South America, while others specialized in mat making, cosmetics, and food production. She supplied guns and ammunition for military expeditions in the hope that the militia would return with enslaved people. She became the leader of her compound, a position usually held by a distinguished male of the lineage. The responsibilities of the lineage included maintaining the compound, providing the commodities for traditional ceremonies, caring for indigent relatives, and overseeing lineage properties. As *iyalode* she held the highest-ranking title a woman could hold. The *iyalode* must have been a proven achiever in business and lineage endeavors; she was the spokesperson for the women traders; and she had a council of female lieutenants. The position of *iyalode* was also a political one; the *iyalode* sat on the male-dominated council of chiefs and

had a voice in law making, the declaration of war, and the general welfare of the community. Her responsibilities extended to the securing of arms and ammunition for the expansionist Ibadan military. Aniwura and the ruler of Ibadan, Arẹ Latoṣa, clashed over the issue of continuous warfare. Her resources were being depleted by the extension of credit to the military, and she was very outspoken in her opposition to Latoṣa's policies. He feared her ability to garner opposition to his policies and is believed to have ordered the *Egungun* Gbajero, a supernatural force embodied by a masquerader who killed women offenders, to brutally murder Aniwura.

There is a legend in which Aniwura was said to have been cruel to those she enslaved, forbidding them to marry and brutally murdering one who became pregnant. Another interpretation of the legend is that, because she was so powerful, few men dared to sexually abuse her enslaved women. Aniwura's oriki—songs which describe the character and achievements of prominent individuals—clearly record her ability to command enormous respect from everyone. A line from her oriki is "the iyalode who instills fear into her equals" (Awẹ 1992, p. 57).

## Chapter 9 (pages 81–88)

1. Robert Armstrong (1981) reported that the people of Oṣogbo "sometimes" regarded the artists who lived there as "quite mad" (p. 53). In 1988, I asked an elderly trader why the artists were considered strange. Her response was that the community did not understand them or the nature of their work.

2. Initially named the Oṣogbo Artist Cooperative, the organization was also known as the Africa Center. On Cooperative letterhead and printed advertisements, personnel were listed as follows: David Osewe, director; Nikẹ Davies, general supervisor; Isaac Ojo Fajana, gallery administrator; Suzanne Wenger, matron; and Jimoh Buraimoh, patron. Davies owned the building and paid for the maintenance and electricity. She restructured the cooperative and changed the name to the Nikẹ Center for Arts and Culture because the senior male artists were advancing their own careers without contributing to the training of the apprentices.

3. Ogundipẹ-Leslie (1993) included women's internalization of low expectations and negative attitudes about the female gender role among the numerous oppressions facing them. In addition to colonialism, neo-colonialism, racism, and traditional sexist behaviors, women's low self-esteem further hampers their progress. "Women are shackled by their own negative self-image, by centuries of the interiorization of the ideologies of patriarchy and gender hierarchy. Their own reactions to objective problems therefore are often self-defeating and self-crippling. Woman reacts with fear, dependency complexes and attitudes to please and cajole rather than where more self-assertive actions are needed" (p. 114).

4. Among the Ibo and Ibibio peoples, twins were considered an abomination. At birth they were immediately put to death or put in a pot and thrown into the bush away from the farmlands. Uka (1966) reported that prejudice against twins still exists in disguised form. Among the Yoruba, twins are celebrated and considered sacred. Their mothers have public permission to solicit alms.

5. For life histories of such women, see Cassiers (1987) and Thompson (1969). Tavy Aherne critiqued the practice of leaving "traditional" artists name-

less and including their works with a "mass of other artists and objects." By guest curating the "Nakunte Diarra: Bogolanfini Artist of the Beledougou" exhibition at the Indiana University Art Museum, January 6–March 7, 1993, Aherne broke with the custom of privileging contemporary African artists with exhibitions of their works. Diarra is a practitioner of the traditionally female art of *bogolanfini*, a mud-dyed cloth of the Bamana region of Mali and a component in marking major life transitions. Aherne emphasized that "traditional" artists are well known in their communities; they have names." Aherne's goal at the exhibition was to allow "the person, the artist to come through. I wanted to give her a name" (*African Studies Program Newsletter*, 1992–93, p. 1).

## Appendix (pages 89–104)

1. There is a belief that of all the elements—earth, fire, air, and water—air is the worst. It is thought that evil-doers take advantage of strong winds to accomplish destructive purposes (Gleason 1992).

2. *Ẹko* is made from maize and is a staple food in the Yoruba diet.

3. *Emere* are thought to have the power to interact with spirits. They are said to have chosen their gift before birth and can use it to evil or good purpose (Gleason 1992).

4. Gammalin 20 is a commonly used pesticide that kills the virus, which destroy crops by attacking the virus's protein coat.

5. The *orisa*, the pantheon of Yoruba deities, are divided into three main groups. The first are those that existed before creation, for example, Ifa, Esu, and Obatala. The second are deified ancestors, for example, Oya, Sango, and Ogun. The third are nature spirits, *imale*, that dwell in ponds, hills, and so on (Lawal 1974). Bello is referring to this third type.

6. Palm oil is used as a pain reliever (Lawal 1974).

7. *Ofun* is a white chalklike substance that is considered both cooling and sanctifying (Gleason 1992). The color white is often associated with water divinities, and stories about heroines' descent under water and return with wealth are common themes of initiation stories (Gorog-Karady 1977).

8. Stories of truth-telling rituals are common among the Yoruba. Orisa Oko, for example, presided over the trials of women accused of witchcraft. The decision was rendered in the cave where the spirit Polo dwelled. Only the accused would enter with Orisa Oko. The spirit would spare the life of the innocent, but the guilty's head would be thrown out to the people waiting for the decision (Johnson 1921/1969).

9. There is a common belief that some women with *aje* kill their children and pretend to cry when the child dies (Hallen and Sodipo 1986).

10. In a study of 240 southwestern Yoruba households in six villages, Adeyemo found that 98 percent of the mothers paid their daughters' school fees, hoping that the girls would pursue professional careers (Adeyemo 1984).

11. The federal government of Nigeria estimates that 65 percent of Nigerian women are illiterate (cited in Osuala 1990). The hardship this poses for Nigerian women in carrying out their roles as wives, mothers, workers, and association members, and the impact on their self-esteem, is poignantly described by Osuala

(1990). Focus group discussions of sixty-two women attending adult literacy classes revealed that they were prevented from obtaining education because (a) fathers chose to educate sons, (b) the girls had to assist their overburdened mothers, or (c) their fathers believed that educating a girl would only enhance her husband's family's well-being or that a woman's education ended in the kitchen. Fathers also married their daughters off young (about age seventeen), before they had a chance to get "spoiled" and damage the family's reputation. To prove their fertility, these women students all had children within a year of their marriages, and most had six children. Without a primary school certificate, these women had only a limited range of jobs available to them: market trading and, less frequently, farming, cooking, hairdressing, tailoring, and employment in churches and hospitals. Osuala concluded that "the inability to read, write and count had been a blight on their lives in countless ways. It had barred them from self-respecting interaction with their fellow-women in social organizations. It had made them feel inferior to their husbands who were more educated than themselves. It had robbed them of their rightful role as educators of their own children. It had stunted their progress in their occupations and undermined their respect for themselves" (p. 97).

12. Fadipẹ (1970) reported that it is one of the new bride's co-wives who pours the water onto the new bride's feet.

13. The privilege to see the new wife's face is purchased with a gift of money (Fadipe 1970).

14. There is a common saying in Nigeria that "it is one's child that keeps a wife in the house of a wicked husband" (Sofola 1992, p. 24).

15. Okediji (1967, 1968) found that as the educational level of a woman increased so did her knowledge of the range of contraceptives available. Women with western-style educations knew about condoms, pills, diaphragms, late weaning, sterilization, and traditional methods such as douching with salt and soap. They learned of these sources through friends but also through books, pharmacists, and family planning clinics. Illiterate women knew primarily about late weaning, withdrawal, and traditional methods. They learned about these methods from friends. The non-educated group of women had an ideal family size of seven, a larger number of living children than the western-educated women, and had negative attitudes toward contraceptive devices and thus tended not to use them. The women without western-style schooling interviewed by Okediji's research assistants tended to reside in unplanned, deteriorated, overcrowded, and unsanitary housing, where pipe-borne water was irregular, malnutrition and malaria frequent, and infant mortality high. Because of "their fate," they regarded a large number of children such as six or more as increasing the odds that some would survive.

16. Bello also added that the other women in her second marriage had many children and she was not sure they knew about family planning. In her first marriage, there were younger wives, notably the sixth wife, who had only two children. I asked Bello why she was not like her. Bello replied that she could not compare herself to this woman, since the woman—though very young when she became a wife—knew many things, because she had been educated. In her first marriage, the women did discuss how to abort children. As soon as they realized they were pregnant they took a combination of alligator pepper (Meleguta) and codeine tablets three times daily for three days. The home remedy was sometimes

effective. Codeine tablets are used as a purgative for stomach ailments affecting women. Alligator pepper is commonly used to cure stomach aches (Buckley 1985).

17. According to Uka (1966), the placenta was wrapped in a white cloth, placed in an earthenware pot, and then buried in the father's compound.

18. It is not unusual for married women to move out of their husband's homes and into their own. Some successful businesswomen even manage to build their own homes, in which they are the sole owners with all rights of senior status accorded them by members of their households (Barnes 1990). Dan Aronson's case study of Madam Bankọle, a Yoruba market woman, described how and why she retained a room in Ibadan during her third marriage although she was residing in northern Nigeria. After she was put out of her marital home during her second marriage, this room provided protection in case things did not go well the third time around. By keeping her license for a market stall in Ibadan, she would always have her trading business and a place to live. When her third husband retired and decided to move from northern Nigeria to Lagos, Bankọle decided for business purposes and to look after her daughter to go and live in her room in Ibadan. In the compound in which she retained a room, seven of the fifteen families were headed by women either temporarily or permanently separated from their husbands (Aronson 1978).

19. In her study of the financial, political, and social benefits of home ownership to Yoruba women, Sandra Barnes (1990) concluded that the major advantage was their ability to control their own time. Discretionary time over and above that devoted to subsistence-producing endeavors was extremely hard to obtain. What most women gain from home ownership, Bello has achieved in living alone. The key is autonomy from domestic demands that obligate a woman's labor and sexual services and emotional energies to others.

# Glossary

*adire* Dyed cloth made through a process of alternating the application of cassava starch or wax and indigo dye

*aje* People with supernatural powers; witchcraft

*akengbe* A calabash

*amu* The large pot women bring to their husband's home that they use for storing drinking water

*babalawo* A priest of the Ifa oracle of divination

*buba* A blouse worn with a wrapper

*ebo* Any sacrifice or offering to the *orisa*s

*Egungun* Refers to concealed powers, specifically supernatural powers, of the ancestors that are invoked to mediate human affairs

*egusi* Melon seed

*eko* A staple food made from maize

*emere*  A human who is thought to be able to communicate with spirits

*gari*  An inexpensive food staple made from cassava

*kobo*  Nigerian currency; it serves the same purpose as the American cent

*imalẹ*  earth spirits

*iya-egbẹ*  A woman who is the leader of her age-group or professional guild

*ilaali*  Henna mixed with water

*mọinọin*  A popular food item made by shelling the skins of beans and then steaming the beans until they form a paste

*naira*  The currency of Nigeria; akin to the dollar; consists of 100 kobo; its value once depended on the international market for oil. Because of Nigeria's Structural Adjustment Program, it has declined in value since its introduction; at one time its strength surpassed the American dollar; at the time of the 1993 interviews, approximately 1 American dollar was equivalent to 40 naira.

*ofun*  A white chalk

*ogi*  A popular food made of fermented corn

*ọja*  Decorative cloth used for carrying babies

*orisạ*  The pantheon of Yoruba deities and deified ancestors

*orogun*  A co-wife; a rival wife

*Oṣogbo*  A traditional Yoruba town in southwestern Nigeria

*Ọṣun*  The female deity of fertility and mythic protector of Oṣogbo

*osun*  A traditional cosmetic derived from the local flora

*ṣigidi*  an image made of mud that is said to have magical properties for protecting and avenging

# References

Abimbọla, W. 1975. *Sixteen Great Poems of Ifa.* Zaria, Nigeria: UNESCO.

Abraham, R. C. 1962. *Dictionary of Modern Yoruba.* London: Hodder and Stoughton.

Abubakr, S. 1992. "Queen Amina of Zaira." In *Nigerian Women in Historical Perspective*, ed. B. Awe, pp. 12–23. Lagos: Sankore Publishers.

Adedeji, J. Y. 1973. "The Literature of the Yoruba Opera." *Spectrum: Monograph Series in the Arts and Sciences, 3*, 55–77.

Adeyemọ, R. 1984. "Women in Rural Areas: A Case Study of Southwestern Nigeria." *Canadian Journal of African Studies, 18*, 563–72.

Afọnja, S. 1989. "Toward the Creation of a New Order for Nigerian Women: Recent Trends in Politics and Policies." *Issue: A Journal of Opinion, 17*, 7–8.

*African Studies Program Newsletter.* Autumn/Winter 1992–93. Bloomington: African Studies Program, Indiana University.

Agheyisi, R. U. 1985. "The Labour Market: Implications of the Access of Women to Higher Education in Nigeria." In *Women in Nigeria Today,* ed. Women in Nigeria Editorial Collective, pp. 143–56. London: Zed Books.

Aidoo, A. A. 1984. "Ghana: To Be a Woman." In *Sisterhood Is Global: The International Women's Movement Anthology*, ed. R. Morgan, pp. 258–65. Garden City: Anchor Press/Doubleday.

Arẹmu, P. S. O. 1991. "Between Myth and Reality: Yoruba Egungun Costumes as Commemorative Clothes." *Journal of Black Studies, 22*, 6–14.

Armstrong, R. P. 1981. *The Powers of Presence: Consciousness, Myth, and Affecting Presence.* Philadelphia: University of Pennsylvania Press.

Aronson, D. R. 1978. *The City Is Our Farm: Seven Migrant Ijebu Yoruba Families.* Cambridge: Schenkman Publishing Company.

Aronson, L. 1984. "Women in the Arts." In *African Women South of the Shara*, ed. M. J. Hay and S. Strichter, pp. 133–37. London: Longman.

————. 1991. "African Women in the Visual Arts: Review Essay." *Signs: A Journal of Women in Culture and Society*, *16*, 550–74.

Awe, B. 1991. "Writing Women into History: The Nigerian Experience." In *Writing Women's History: International Perspectives*, ed. K. Offen, R. Pierson, and J. Rendall, pp. 211–20. Bloomington: Indiana University Press.

————. 1992. "Iyalode Ẹfunṣẹtan Aniwura" [Owner of Gold]. In *Nigerian Women in Historical Perspective*, ed. B. Awe, pp. 55–71. Lagos: Sankore Publishers, Ltd.

Badejọ, D. L. 1989. "The Goddess Ọṣun as a Paradigm for African Feminist Criticism." *Sage: A Scholarly Journal about Black Women*, *6*, 27–32.

Barnes, S. T. 1986. *Patrons and Power: Creating a Political Community in Metropolitan Lagos*. Bloomington: Indiana University Press.

————. 1990. "Women, Property, and Power." In *Beyond the Second Sex: New Directions in the Anthropology of Gender*, ed. P. R. Sanday and R. G. Goodenough, pp. 256–80. Philadelphia: University of Pennsylvania Press.

Bascom, W. R. 1941. "The Sanctions of Ifa Divination." *Journal of the Royal Anthropological Institute*, *71*, 43–53.

————. 1942. "The Principal of Seniority in the Social Structure of the Yoruba," *American Anthropologist*, *44*, 37–46.

————. 1951a. "Yoruba Food." *Africa*, *21*, 41–53.

————. 1951b. "Yoruba Cooking." *Africa*, *21*, 125–37.

Beier, U. 1991. *Thirty Years of Oshogbo Art*. Lagos: IWALEWA House Bayreuth in cooperation with Goethe Institute.

Belasco, B. I. 1980. *The Entrepreneur as Culture Hero: Preadaptations in Nigerian Economic Development*. New York: Praeger Publishers.

Buckley, A. D. 1985. *Yoruba Medicine*. Oxford: Clarendon Press.

Butler, D. A. 1986."Batiks from the Oshun." *West Africa*, March 17, p. 72.

Cassiers, A. 1987. "Mercha: An Ethopian Woman Speaks of Her Life." In *Life Histories of African Women*, ed. Patricia Romero, pp. 159–93. London: Ashfield.

Clegg, S. 1987. "Nigerian Shares Her Art, Culture." *Calgary Herald*, April 5, p. 54.

Dalziel, J. M. 1937/1955. *The Useful Plants of West Tropical Africa*. London: Crown Agents for Overseas Governments and Administrations.

Delano, I. O. 1973. "Proverbs, Songs, and Poems." In *Sources of Yoruba History*, ed. S. O. Biobaku, pp. 77–85. London: Oxford University Press.

de Negri, E. 1976. *Nigerian Body Adornment*. Lagos: Academy Press.

Dennett, R. E. 1910, 1968. *Nigerian Studies of the Religious and Political System of the Yoruba*. London: Frank Cass & Company.

Dorkenoo, E., and S. Elworthy. 1992. *Female Genital Mutilation: Proposals for Change*. Manchester: Manchester Free Press.

Drewal, H. J. 1989. "Art or Accident: Yoruba Body Artists and Their Deity Ogun." In *Africa's Ogun: Old World and New*, ed. S. T. Barnes, pp. 235–60. Bloomington: Indiana University Press.

Drewal, M. 1992. *Yoruba Ritual: Performers, Play, Agency*. Bloomington: Indiana University Press.

Eades, J. S. 1980. *The Yoruba Today*. Cambridge: Cambridge University Press.

Eicher, J. B. 1976. *Nigerian Handcrafted Textiles*. Ile-Ife, Nigeria: University of Ife Press.

Ellis, A. B. 1894/1964. *The Yoruba-Speaking Peoples of the Slave Coast of West Africa: Their Religion, Manners, Customs, Laws, Language, etc.* Chicago: Benin Press.

Entwisle, B., and C. Coles. 1990. "Demographic Surveys and Nigerian Women." *Signs: A Journal of Women in Culture and Society*, *15*, 259–84.

Fadipẹ, N. A. 1970. *The Sociology of the Yoruba*. Ibadan, Nigeria: University Of Ibadan Press.

Fikry-Atallah, M. 1972. "Wala Oral History and Wa's Social Realities." In *African Folklore*, ed. R. Dorson, pp. 405–7. Garden City: Anchor Books.

Froula, C. 1986. "The Daughter's Seduction: Sexual Violence and Literary History." *Signs: A Journal of Women in Culture and Society*, *11*, 621–44.

Gibson, E. 1981. "Nigerian Artists Portray Traditions in Western Context." *Denton Record Chronicle*, March 27, 1B.

Gleason, J. 1992. *Oya: In Praise of an African Goddess*. San Francisco: Harper.

Gorog-Karady, V. 1977. "Parental Preference and Racial Inequality: An Ideological Theme in African Oral Literature." In *Forms of Folklore in Africa: Narrative, Poetic, Gnomic, Dramatic*, ed. B. Lindfors, pp. 104–34. Austin: University of Texas Press.

Graham-White, A. 1974. "Yoruba Opera: Developing a New Drama for the Nigerian People." *Theatre Quarterly*, *14*, 33–41.

Hallen, B., and J. O. Ṣodipọ. 1986. *Knowledge, Belief and Witchcraft: Analytic Experiments in African Philosophy*. London: Ethnographica.

Hoch-Smith, J. 1978. "Radical Yoruba Female Sexuality: The Witch and the Prostitute." In *Women in Ritual and Symbolic Roles*, ed. J. Hoch-Smith and A. Spring, pp. 245–67. New York: Plenum Press.

Hodder, B. W. 1962. "The Yoruba Rural Market." In *Markets in Africa*, ed. P. Bohannan and G. Dalton, pp. 103–17. Evanston: Northwestern University Press.

Hosken, F. 1982. *The Hosken Report—Genital Mutilation of Females*. Lexington: Women's International Network News.

Jẹgẹdẹ, D. 1984. "Patronage and Change in Nigerian Art." *Nigeria Magazine*, *150*, 29–36.

Jeyifọ, B. 1984. *The Yoruba Popular Travelling Theatre of Nigeria*. Lagos: Department of Culture, Federal Ministry of Social Development, Youth, Sports, and Culture.

Johnson, S. 1921/1969. *The History of the Yorubas*. London: Routledge and Kegan Paul.

Kanyogonya, E. 1986. "Akina Mama wa Afrika." *African Concord*, March 20, p. 40.

Kennedy, J. 1968. "I Saw and I Was Happy: Festival at Oshogbo." *African Arts*, *1*, 8–17, 85.

King, N. Q. 1986. *African Cosmos: An Introduction to Religion in Africa*. Belmont, CA: Wadsworth Publishing Company.

LaDuke B. 1991. *Africa Through the Eyes of Women Artists*. Trenton: African World Press.

Lawal, B. 1974. "Some Aspects of Yoruba Aesthetics." *British Journal of Aesthetics*, *14*, 239–49.

LeVine, B. B. 1962. *Yoruba Students' Memories of Childhood Rewards and Punishments* (Interim Report). Ibadan: University of Ibadan, Institute of Education, Ibadan University Press.

LeVine, R. A., H. H. Klein, and C. R. Owen. 1967. "Father–Child Relationships and Changing Life Styles in Ibadan, Nigeria." In *The City in Modern Africa*, ed. H. Miner, pp. 215–55. London: Pall Mall Press.

Lloyd, P. C. 1968. "Divorce among the Yoruba." *American Anthropologist, 70*, 67–81.

Maclean, U. 1982. "Folk Medicine and Fertility: Aspects of Yoruba Medical Practice Affecting Women." In *Ethnography of Fertility and Birth*, ed. C. P. MacCormack, pp. 161–79. London: Academic Press.

Makinde, M. A. 1988. *African Philosophy, Culture and Traditional Medicine*. Athens: Ohio University Center for International Studies, Africa Series #53.

Matory, J. L. 1994. *Sex and the Empire that Is No More: Gender and the Politics of Metaphor in Ọyọ Yoruba Religion*. Minnesota: University of Minnesota Press.

Mugambi, S. 1992. "Adire Art." *Rainbow*, May, pp. 12–13.

Obbo, C. 1975." Women's Careers in Low Income Areas as Indicators of Country and Town Dynamics." In *Town and Country in Central and Eastern Africa*, ed. D. Parkin, pp. 288–93. Oxford: Oxford University Press for International African Institute.

———. 1980. *African Women: Their Struggle for Economic Indepencence*. London: Zed Press.

Ọdẹbiyi, D. 1981. "Meet Nikẹ, the Artist." *Lagos Weekend*, December 11, p. 8.

Ogundipẹ, A. 1978. *Eṣu Ẹlẹgbara, the Yoruba God of Chance and Uncertainity: A Study in Yoruba Mythology*. Doctoral dissertation, Bloomington: Indiana University.

Ogundipẹ-Leslie, M. 1992. "Beyond Hearsay and Academic Journalism: The Black Woman and Ali Mazuri." Paper presented at the African Studies Association Conference, Seattle, Washington, November 20–23.

———. 1993. "African Women, Culture and Another Development." In *Theorizing Black Feminisms: The Visionary Pragmatism of Black Women*, ed. S. James and A. P. A. Abusia, pp. 102–17. New York: Routledge.

Ojo, G. J. A. 1966. *Yoruba Culture: A Geographic Analysis*. London: University of London Press.

Okediji, F. O. 1967. "Some Social Psychological Aspects of Fertility Among Married Women in an African City." *The Nigerian Journal of Economic and Social Studies, 9*, 67–79.

———. 1968. "Attitude, Knowledge and Practice of Family Planning Techniques Among Married Women in the City of Ibadan." *The West African Medical Journal and Nigerian Practioner, 17*, 211–18.

Okonjo, K. 1991. "Rural Development in Nigeria: How Do Women Count?" In *Women in Nigerian Economy*, ed. M. O. Ijere, pp. 184–211. Enugu, Nigeria: Acena Publishers.

Olusanya, G. O. 1992. "Ọlaniwun Adunni Oluwọle." In *Nigerian Women in Historical Perspective*, ed. B. Ạwe, pp. 123–31. Lagos: Sankore Publishers.

Osuala, J. D. C. 1990. "Nigerian Women's Quest for Role Fulfillment." *Women and Therapy*, *10*, 89–98.

Oyẹṣakin, A. 1987. "Women as Agents of Indiscipline." *Nigeria Magazine*, *53*, 38–43.

Plotnicov, L. 1967. *Strangers to the City: Urban Man in Jos, Nigeria*. Pittsburgh: University of Pittsburgh Press.

Porrelli, C. 1983. "Nigerian Batik Artist Creates Colorful Works at Country Fair." *Los Angeles Tribune*, October 2, p. E1.

Press, R. 1992. "One Teacher's Devotion to Art." *Christian Science Monitor*, November 3, p. 10.

———. 1992. "Africa in Blue." *Christian Science Monitor*, September 25, pp. 10–11.

Prince, R. 1961. "The Yoruba Image of the Witch." *Journal of Mental Science*, *107*, 795–805.

———. 1964. "Indigenous Yoruba Psychiatry." In *Magic, Faith, and Healing*, ed. A. Kiev, pp. 84–120. New York: Free Press.

Roberts, J. W. 1989. *From Trickster to Badman: The Black Folk Hero in Slavery and Freedom*. Philadelphia: University of Pennsylvania Press.

Schildkrout, E. 1987. "Hajiya Husaina: Notes on the Life History of a Hausa Woman." In *Life Histories of African Women*, ed. P. Romero, pp. 78–79. London: Ashfield.

Scott, V. 1983. "Nikẹ Ọlaniyi." *African Arts*, *16*, 46–47.

Simpson, G. E. 1980. *Yoruba Religion and Medicine in Ibadan*. Ibadan: Ibadan University Press.

Sofola, Z. 1992. "Feminism and the Psyche of African Womanhood." Paper presented at Women in Africa and the African Diaspora: Bridges across Activism and the Academy Nssuka, Enugu State, Nigeria, July 13–18.

Ṣowande, E. J. 1913, 1991. *A Dictionary of the Yoruba Language*. Ibadan: University Press.

Ṣoyinka, W. 1988. *Aké: The Childhood Years*. Ibadan: Spectrum.

Staff. 1985a. "Nigerian Pearl at Edinburgh Festival." *The Guardian*, August 7, p. 10.

———. 1985b. "Magazine Hosts Gala Ball for Delegates." *Daily Nation*, July 26, p. 10.

Stone, R. H. 1899. *In Africa's Forest and Jungle: Or, Six Years Among the Yorubans*. New York: Fleming H. Revell Company.

Talbot, P. A. 1926, 1969. *The Peoples of Southern Nigeria*, 4 vols. London: Frank Cass & Company.

Thompson, R. F. 1969. "Abatan: A Master Potter of the Ẹgbado Yoruba." In *Tradition and Creativity in Tribal Art*, ed. D. Biebuyck, pp. 120–83. Berkeley: University of California Press.

Tutuọla, A. 1953. *The Palm-Wine Drinkard*. New York: Grove Press.

Uka, N. 1966. *Growing Up in Nigerian Culture: A Pioneer Study of Physical and Behavioural Growth and Development of Nigerian Children*. Occasional publication. University of Ibadan, Institute of Education.

Verger, P. 1971. "Tranquilizers and Stimulants in Yoruba Herbal Treatment." In *The Traditional Background to Medical Practice in Nigeria*, ed. R. Armstrong, pp. 50–60. [Occasional publication #25.] Ibadan: University of Ibadan.

Walker, A. 1982. *The Color Purple*. New York: Washington Square Press.

Ware, H. 1979. "Polygyny: Women's Views in a Transitional Society, Nigeria 1975." *Journal of Marriage and the Family, 41*, 185–95.

Waterman, C. A. 1990. *Jùjú: A Social History and Ethnography of an African Popular Music*. Chicago: University of Chicago Press.

Zamana Gallery. 1988. *Contemporary Arts from Western Nigeria: The Oshogbo School*. London: Zamana Gallery.

# Index

**Kim Marie Vaz** received her doctorate in educational psychology with a minor in African Studies from Indiana University, Bloomington. Currently, she is an assistant professor of Women's Studies at the University of South Florida in Tampa. She is the editor of *Black Women in America* (1995) and has been a contributor to *Spirit, Space and Survival: Black Women in (White) Academe* (1993), *Women's Studies Quarterly*, and *Women and Therapy: A Feminist Journal.* She is a co-producer of a documentary video entitled "Spirit Murder: Stopping the Violent Deaths of Black Women" (University of South Florida's Video and Film Distribution Center, Division of Learning Technologies, Tampa, FL 33620).